PORTRAIT OF THE
Welsh Highland Railway

Peter Johnson

Ian Allan
PUBLISHING

Front cover: One of the North Wales Narrow Gauge Railways' single Fairlies at Rhyd Ddu. *Peacock/Gwyn Price Collection*

Back cover top: Two NGG16 Garratts approach Hendy Crossing on the Welsh Highland Railway (Caernarfon) on 20 September 1998. The Pullman car is coupled behind the locomotives. *Peter Johnson*

Back cover bottom: A map, published in 1923, showing how the Welsh Highland, Festiniog and Snowdon Mountain Railways, then under common management, related to each other. *Commercial postcard/Peter Treloar Collection*

Title page: Gowrie with a goods train at Dinas, c1911. *G. M. Perkins/Adrian Gray Collection*

Below: What appears to be a late use of the standard gauge crossing by a passenger train, in 1936. *S. W. Baker/WHR(P)*

Below right: A map of the WHR published in 1923. *Railway Magazine*

First published 1999
Revised reprint 2000

ISBN 0 7110 2658 0

Published by Ian Allan Publishing

an imprint of Ian Allan Publishing Ltd, Terminal House, Station Approach, Shepperton, Surrey TW17 8AS.

Printed by Ian Allan Printing Ltd, Riverdene Business Park, Hersham, Surrey KT12 4RG.

Code: 0005/3

Note — Welsh names
While it is usual now for proper names in Wales to be given their correct Welsh spellings, this was not always the case. In this book legal names and titles are presented in their original archaic forms; for place names the Welsh form is used throughout except where quoted. For example, in an Act of Parliament Caernarfon is Carnarvon, until 1974 the County Council was 'Caernarvonshire' but the geographical entity is always Caernarfon.

Contents

Introduction   5

Acknowledgements   6

Bibliography   7

1. The Nantlle Tramway   9

2. The Croesor Tramway   13

3. The North Wales Narrow Gauge Railways   19

4. The Portmadoc, Beddgelert   41
    & South Snowdon Railway

5. The Welsh Highland Railway 1921-44   47

6. Welsh Highland Railway Revival —   91
    To the Millennium

Parliamentary Powers   111

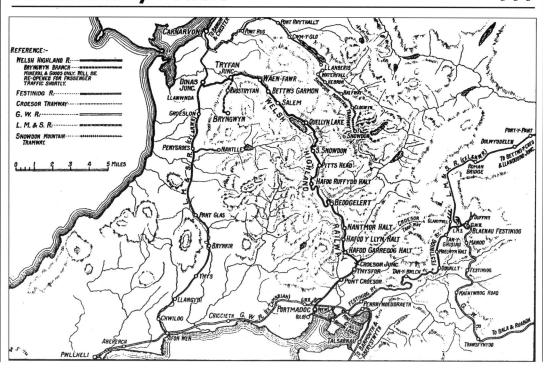

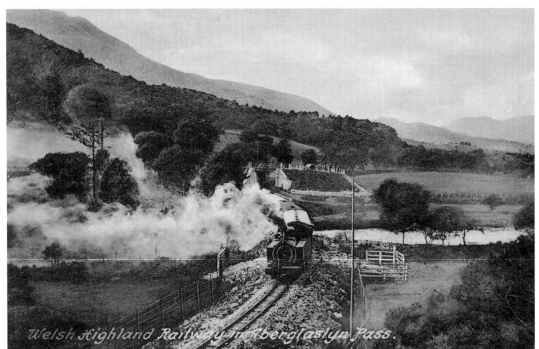

Welsh Highland Railway in Aberglaslyn Pass.

Introduction

There can be no doubt about it. The restoration of the Welsh Highland Railway is one of the Holy Grails of railway preservation. Though it might have appeared to have been an unattainable objective for so many years, the pieces of the jigsaw are at last coming together to make the revived Welsh Highland Railway a reality.

The Welsh Highland Railway route itself has one of the most complex histories of any narrow gauge line. The narrow gauge railway link between Caernarfon and Porthmadog, a dream since the mid-1850s, almost became reality in 1923. At this time the completion of the Rhyd Ddu-Croesor Junction link line between the North Wales Narrow Gauge Railways and the upgraded Croesor Tramway from Croesor Junction to Porthmadog, provided a route which, terminating at Dinas Junction, almost reached Caernarfon, some three miles away. Only in the 21st century, it seems, will the dream of a Caernarfon-Porthmadog railway become an actuality.

Complexity is contributed to the story by more than 20 Parliamentary Acts and Orders obtained in relation to various parts of the route, few of which dealt with it in its entirety; not to mention that the North Wales Narrow Gauge Railways became moribund in the 1910s. Attempts by that company to build an extension to Beddgelert, and by the Portmadoc, Beddgelert & South Snowdon Railway to build the link line were both abandoned, the PBSSR leaving incomplete earthworks which are still to be seen today. The WHR itself was not operated after 1937, its track was requisitioned for the war effort in 1941 and it has been in receivership since 1944. To add

further variety, the Dinas-Caernarfon section was authorised at least four times and has been operated on three different gauges!

Despite the comparatively recent implementation of the 1923 through route, the prehistory and early history of elements of it include the involvement of such famous names as the Stephenson brothers, Thomas Savin, Charles Easton Spooner and Col Stephens. Spooner's participation explains the early involvement of the Festiniog Railway in the route, with leasing and operating powers being awarded at various times, culminating in the Welsh Highland and the FR coming under common management in 1921 and then the FR leasing the Welsh Highland in 1934.

Attempts to preserve and restore the Welsh Highland Railway were first given formal status by the registration of the Welsh Highland Light Railway (1964) Co Ltd, which later became established on the site of the standard gauge Beddgelert Siding at Porthmadog. While this company was unsuccessful in wresting the trackbed from the Official Receiver, it did succeed in raising the profile of the trackbed as the site of a railway to be reinstated, preventing its being taken over for other purposes.

Progress in restoring the railway was made, however, when the Festiniog Railway again took an interest, although on this occasion not without some considerable controversy.

The Festiniog concept is for a 40-mile narrow gauge railway from Caernarfon to Blaenau Ffestiniog, completing the route of Spooner's vision by starting within sight of the famous castle walls at Caernarfon and reinstating the cross-town link at Porthmadog. Having secured a grant from the Millennium Commission, the first stage — Caernarfon to Dinas — was brought into use in October 1997. The line to Porthmadog should be completed before the 10th anniversary of the publication of this book. With the prospect of Garratts working 12-coach trains on the reverse curves of the 1 in 40 gradients around Beddgelert and through the Aberglaslyn Pass, the Welsh Highland Railway is surely a Holy Grail worth fighting for.

Above left: Russell and *Beddgelert* were almost synonymous with the WHR. The train of NWNGR coaches is seen on an overcast day, with passengers conspicuous by their absence.
W. G. Rear Collection/WHR(P)

Below left: Russell at Bryn-y-felin, c1924.
Frith/Peter Johnson Collection

Acknowledgements

In reading this book it will be seen that the Welsh Highland Railway has been, and will be, no ordinary railway and, for me, this has been no ordinary book. For one thing, the railway is still under construction and at the time of writing, for want of the decision on the Transport & Works Order application, its future is less clear than it might be. For another, I had the task (at the end satisfactory if not always straightforward) of producing, voluntarily, numerous drafts of that Order. In becoming, also, effectively the project photographer during the 1997 construction phase, I gained a valuable insight into developments as they happened. I hope, therefore, that I have been able to present a clear account of this stage of the railway's development, despite it still being subject to change as this book goes through its production process.

I wish to take this opportunity of wholeheartedly acknowledging the warm welcome I received from all involved in the construction of the Dinas-Caernarfon section of the re-created Welsh Highland Railway during 1997. Their willingness to explain what was going on and to endure the photographic process was exemplary. Behind the scenes and in the office Mike Hart, Michael Schumann, Tony Smare, Michael Pritchard, Roland Doyle, Jan Woods and Maddy Chester were always willing to answer questions and provide background briefings.

Writing this book has been a great pleasure, especially as new photographs and information came to light, as work progressed in a manner totally unexpected when I began. I especially appreciate the enthusiasm and support received from David Allan, Michael Bishop, Maurice Done, Bob Gartside, Adrian Gray, Paul Ingham, Peter Jarvis, David Johnson (Millbrook House, and still no relation), John Keylock, Gwyn Price, Bill Rear, Peter Treloar, Rodney Weaver and Michael Whitehouse, to whom I am greatly indebted. The staff at Gwynedd Archives performed a valuable service in retrieving documents relating to Caernarvonshire County Council's involvement with the WHR. The editor of *Railway Magazine* kindly sanctioned use of a map first used in that organ's pages.

Members of the Welsh Highland Railway Ltd (formerly WHLR [1964] Co) have spent many years collecting photographs of the Welsh Highland Railway and its predecessors, some of which are reproduced here. Copies of the WHR Ltd collection are on sale and details can be obtained from Welsh Highland Railway Ltd, Porthmadog LL49 9DY.

Welsh Highland Heritage is responsible for documenting and preserving WHR history and artefacts, and publishes a quarterly newsletter. Membership details can be obtained from Welsh Highland Heritage, Weathervane Cottage, Childswickham, Broadway WR12 7HL.

The Welsh Highland Railway Society exists to support the reconstruction and operation of the Welsh Highland Railway/Rheilffordd Eryri. It co-ordinates volunteer activity and publishes a quarterly magazine. Members also receive travel privileges. Details are available from the Society at PO Box 1590, Caernarfon LL55 2WE.

During the course of compiling this book I have been pleased to have access to background documents relating to the Welsh Highland Railway, some of which appear not to have been examined by those writing on this complex subject in the past. This has allowed re-examination of some aspects to be undertaken. It goes without saying that any misinterpretation or errors of fact remain my responsibility.

Peter Johnson
Leicester, March 1999

Events 1999/2000

Eryri Local Plan — in his report submitted on 21 January 1999, the inspector concluded that 'reinstatement of the WHR was in the public interest and does not conflict with National Park purposes'.

Welsh Highland Railway Transport & Works Order — the Order (1999/2129) was made on 30 June 1999 and came into effect on 21 July 1999. Work started to clear the trackbed between Waunfawr and Dinas in October. In March 2000 the 27 May target for re-opening was deferred to 14 July due to exceptionally wet winter delaying progress. The summer of 2001 is now the target for re-opening to Rhyd Ddu.

Bontnewydd Halt — in response to a request from local residents a halt was opened at Bontnewydd on 29 May 1999.

Locomotive movements — to contain operating expenses the Festiniog Railway's 2-4-0STT *Blanche* was transferred to Dinas on 13 May 1999. After trials it commenced working weekday passenger services on 7 June, hauling a three-coach train, remaining in
service until the end of the season. In March 2000 it was returned to Boston Lodge for boiler repairs, being replaced by Alco 2-6-2T *Mountaineer*, now in lined black livery. Planet 4-wheeled diesel *Conway Castle* was transported to Dinas at the same time, providing back-up for Funkey *Castell Caernarfon* whilst *Upnor Castle* was isolated from the main line whilst working construction trains.

Millennium postage stamp issue — the Royal Mail's 2000 stamp issue featured projects supported by the Millennium Commission. On 1 February a 26p issue featured Garratt No 143; it was a composite view, the locomotive and train were photographed approaching St Helen's Road Bridge whilst the backdrop was photographed near Rhyd Ddu.

6

Bibliography

Baughan, Peter E.; *A Regional History of the Railways of Great Britain; Vol 11 North and Mid Wales*; David St John Thomas, 2nd edition 1991

Boyd, J. I. C.; *Narrow Gauge Railways in North Caernarvonshire; Vol 1 West*; Oakwood Press, 1981

Boyd, J. I. C.; *Narrow Gauge Railways in South Caernarvonshire*, Oakwood Press, 1988/9 (2 vols)

Bradley, V. J.; *Industrial Locomotives of North Wales*; Industrial Railway Society, 1992

Christiansen, Rex; *Forgotten Railways North and Mid Wales*; David & Charles, 2nd edition 1984

David, Trefor; *Tickets of the North Wales Narrow Gauge Railway*; Welsh Highland Heritage, 1999

Johnson, Peter; *Portrait of the Festiniog*; Ian Allan, 1992

Johnson, Peter; 'The Welsh Highland Railway — a narrow gauge epic', *Steam Railway*; January 1998

Lee, Charles E.; *Narrow Gauge Railways in North Wales*; Railway Publishing Co, 1945

Millard, Keith & Booth, Peter; *Welsh Highland Railway Rolling Stock Drawings*; 7mm Narrow Gauge Association

Mitchell, Vic & Smith, Keith; *Branch lines around Portmadoc — the Welsh Highland and Festiniog Railways 1923-46*; Middleton Press, 1993

Mitchell, Vic & Smith, Keith; *Branch lines around Porthmadog — the Welsh Highland and Festiniog Railways 1954-94*; Middleton Press, 1994

Rear, W. G.; *LMS Branch lines in North Wales*; Wild Swan Publications, 1986

Rear, W. G.; *Caernarvon and the Lines from Afon Wen and Llanberis*; Foxline Publishing, 1996

Rheilffordd Eryri The Welsh Highland Railway; Festiniog Railway Co, 1994

Stretton, John; *The Festiniog and Welsh Highland Railways*; Past & Present Publishing, 1996

Thomas, Dewi W.; *Hydro-electricity in North West Wales*; National Power plc, 1997

Vignes, Edouard (English translation by D. A. Boreham); *A Technical Study of the Festiniog & Other Narrow-Gauge Railways 1878*; P. E. Waters & Associates, 1986

The Welsh Highland Railway — the Ffestiniog Railway's proposals; Festiniog Railway Co, 1992

Above: The WHR sign by the main Caernarfon-Lleyn road obviously had some significance for the unknown photographer and the young ladies. Regrettably it had little influence on the railway's fortunes. *FR Archives*

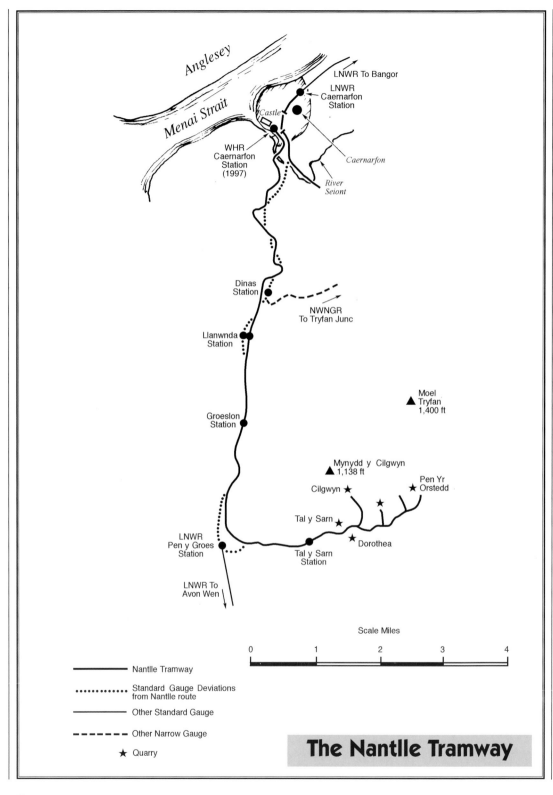

Anglesey

Menai Strait

LNWR To Bangor

LNWR
Caernarfon
Station

Castle

WHR
Caernarfon
Station
(1997)

Caernarfon

*River
Seiont*

Dinas
Station

NWNGR
To Tryfan Junc

Llanwnda
Station

▲ Moel
Tryfan
1,400 ft

Groeslon
Station

Mynydd y Cilgwyn
▲ 1,138 ft

Cilgwyn ★

Pen Yr
★ Orstedd

Tal y Sarn ★

LNWR
Pen y Groes
Station

★ Dorothea

Tal y Sarn
Station

LNWR To
Avon Wen

Scale Miles

| 0 | 1 | 2 | 3 | 4 |

———— Nantlle Tramway

•••••••••• Standard Gauge Deviations
from Nantlle route

———— Other Standard Gauge

– – – – – Other Narrow Gauge

★ Quarry

The Nantlle Tramway

The Nantlle Tramway

Most of the first section of the re-created Welsh Highland Railway to be brought into use, Caernarfon-Dinas, has the distinction of being the oldest part of the route.

The Nantlle Tramway was a 3ft 6in gauge horse tramway connecting slate quarries in the Nantlle vale with the port at Caernarfon, a distance of about 8 miles. Pre-dating even the Ffestiniog line, it was incorporated by an Act of 1825 and opened in 1828.

Below: A typical Nantlle Tramway train, photographed at Talysarn on 20 April 1957. The wagons were typical of the Nantlle throughout its history. Notice the double-flanged wheels.
W. A. Camwell/W. G. Rear Collection

Quarrying in the Nantlle vale was long established but not by monopolistic owners on the scale of Penrhyn or Dinorwic, or even Blaenau Ffestiniog. There were many quarries exploited at different times on varying scales, with varying degrees of success, rendering co-operation to provide communal transportation difficult. However, the construction of the Dinorwic Railway, completed in 1824, brought the threat of cut-price competition and provided the impetus the Nantlle proprietors needed to improve their own transport links.

In 1825 some 30 interested persons agreed to subscribe £20,000 in £100 shares for a railway and a successful application was made to Parliament. The use of stationary steam engines was sanctioned. Haulage, however, was to be by

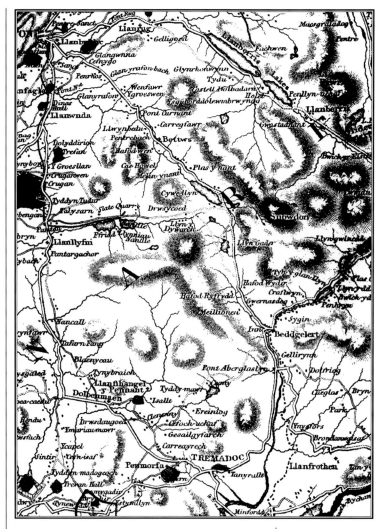

Left: A map showing the WHR route district in 1830/1, when the Nantlle Tramway was the only railway in the area.
C. & J. Greenwood/ Peter Johnson Collection

Right: At Caernarfon the Nantlle Tramway ran along the street, past the de Winton factory, extreme right. The train on the disused Afon Wen line formed an Investiture Day special on 1 July 1969. *A. Wyn Hobson/ W. G. Rear Collection*

Below right: The Nantlle Tramway terminated at Caernarfon Quay, in front of the castle, an industrial site until the 1950s, when it began to be used for parking. The 1997 railway is to be extended to the site alongside the locomotive. *W. G. Rear*

horse power. Brothers George and Robert Stephenson played a consultancy role during construction. Robert is known to have visited the locality to investigate availability of track materials and other matters in 1827. Further Acts of Parliament were obtained in 1827, authorising additional funding, and in 1828, authorising further time for construction. With some work still outstanding, it was possible to open the line on 17 July that year.

The Nantlle Tramway was operated with the quarry owners/operators themselves providing their own horses and wagons, paying tolls for the privilege. There were 22 passing places along the single line. Passengers were carried officially from 1856, although there appeared to be some doubt about the legitimacy of this provision. Additional to the terminals there were stations at

Bontnewydd, Pwllheli Road (Llanwnda), Groeslon and Pen-y-groes. Passenger runs were timetabled to take 90min against the grade to Nantlle and about 10min less in the reverse direction. Some goods workings could be expected to take nearly four hours.

Proposals to build a standard gauge railway between Caernarfon and Porthmadog came to a head with the Parliamentary establishment of the Carnarvonshire Railway in 1862. This incorporated the Nantlle for most of its route, from Caernarfon to Pen-y-groes, and joined it to a new line thence to Afon Wen. The Festiniog Railway's Charles Easton Spooner became engineer in 1864 — his activities were to be pivotal in the development of what became the Welsh Highland Railway. The infamous Thomas Savin, a shareholder, was appointed contractor.

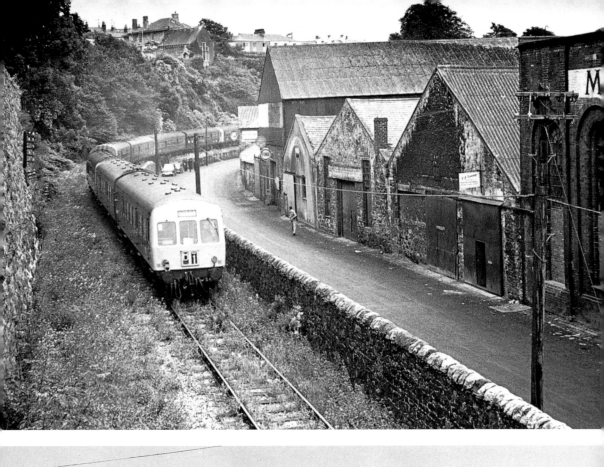

Left: The Nantlle Tramway tunnel under Coed Helen Road at Caernarfon, seen on 23 August 1997. The observant/informed may notice the far end portal from the train as they pass under the former standard gauge bridge at the same location. A second Nantlle tunnel survives under the road to Plas Dinas. *Peter Johnson*

(This account is necessarily a simplistic one. A great deal of politicking was carried out by all participants as well as the Aberystwyth & Welsh Coast Railway and the London & North Western Railway, but is outside the scope of this book.)

The Nantlle Railway Act of 1865 authorised additional capital and new 3ft 6in lines coinciding with the Carnarvonshire Railway's proposals, plus a branch from Nantlle to a terminus near Rhyd Ddu. Provided it was not greater than standard gauge, the gauge could be increased at any time. These powers of gauge conversion may have been used in preference to those of the Carnarvonshire Railway's for a new line between Pen-y-groes and Caernarfon.

However, Spooner had reported good progress being made on the Coed Helen to Pen-y-groes section just before Savin was declared bankrupt in 1866. The latter owned nearly three-quarters of the £200,000 authorised share capital. A Bill to vest the Nantlle undertaking in the Carnarvonshire was enacted in 1867. The Act's preamble justified it thus:

'And whereas there subsists between the Undertaking of the Nantlle Company and the Undertaking of the Carnarvonshire Company a close connection for the purpose of traffic, and it would conduce to the public convenience if the Undertaking of the Nantlle Company were vested in the Carnarvonshire Company, and the both companies are desirous that such a vesting should be effected upon the conditions in this Act contained.'

At that time the standard gauge terminated at a temporary station near Pant Farm, the location now better known as Hendy Crossing, pending construction of the viaduct across the Afon Seiont into Caernarfon. Nantlle traffic consequently underwent a change of gauge at both Pen-y-groes and Pant, to its considerable inconvenience and expense.

During the 1860s negotiations with the Carnarvon & Llanberis Railway (C&LR) concerning joint access and a shared station in Caernarfon took place, being agreed in the C&LR's 1864 Act, modified in the C&LR's 1865 Act and repealed in the C&LR's 1867 Act! Eventually the two railways had separate parallel lines into the town. Had the C&LR's 1864 route been built, the Harbour Trustees would have built a tramway between the C&LR's terminus and the existing Bangor & Carnarvon Railway station, to be shared by the C&LR and the Nantlle Tramway.

The London & North Western Railway exercised its powers to absorb the Carnarvonshire Railway in 1870. The Afon Seiont viaduct completed, a nominal junction with the Carnarvon & Llanberis Railway on the northern bank of the river brought the standard gauge line into Caernarfon, although each line had its own track through to the town station. To facilitate continued use of the harbour, a connection was formed between the Carnarvonshire Railway and sidings laid on the wharf by the harbour trustees, the junction being located close to the 1997 narrow gauge railway terminus.

On the former Nantlle section, curves were eased or bypassed to accommodate the standard gauge. Despite the long period out of use, some remarkable relics of the original Nantlle route still survive, notably tunnels at Coed Helen and Plas Dinas, and the river bridge at Bontnewydd. The last remnant of the horse-worked 3ft 6in gauge line, then owned by British Railways, continued in use until closure in 1963, the last user being Pen-yr-orsedd Quarry. The standard gauge line closed in 1964, the trackbed being bought by the then Caernarvonshire County Council and converted to a long-distance cycle track called Lôn Eifion.

The Croesor Tramway

Another part of the Porthmadog-Caernarfon route also has its origins in a horse tramway. The Croesor Tramway was a 2ft gauge horse tramway built privately in 1864 to link quarries in the remote Croesor valley with Porthmadog. The valley lies north of and parallel to the vale of Ffestiniog, the vale providing the outlet for Blaenau Ffestiniog slate production, originally by the Afon Dwyryd and then the Festiniog Railway. High and impossibly steep ground prevented transport links being established between the Croesor valley and the Ffestiniog Railway, on the opposite side of the Moelwyns.

The tramway's proprietor was Hugh Beaver Roberts, a successful solicitor practising in Bangor. He had interests in several North Wales quarries, in some cases extending those interests into providing rail links for their output, as will be seen. In the Croesor he was a landowner, owning the land on which were located several quarries, including the Croesor Fawr Slate Quarrying Co Ltd of which he was a director.

No Parliamentary powers were obtained to authorise the tramway's construction, Roberts obtaining wayleaves to secure its right of way where he did not already own the land. Charles Easton Spooner was again involved, surveying the route in 1863. In the valley private tramways and inclines made connections to the main line. At Porthmadog agreement was given for use of the Ffestiniog's tracks around the harbour, on payment of 3d [1] per ton on opening, later reduced to 1½d per ton.

The position was regularised in 1865, with the passing of the Croesor & Portmadoc Railway Act. The Act incorporated the Croesor & Portmadoc Railway Co (CPRC) having share capital of £25,000 in £50 shares. The tramway, called 'the railway' in the Act, was vested in the company and was authorised to be used for passenger traffic as well as mineral and goods traffic. The route was defined as 'the existing Railway which

[1] *Three old pence (pre-1971 decimalisation) of which there were 12 to the shilling (s) and 20 shillings to the pound.*

Below: A map used by the Festiniog Railway in its promotional material, showing the Croesor Tramway as well as the standard gauge connections.
Peter Johnson Collection

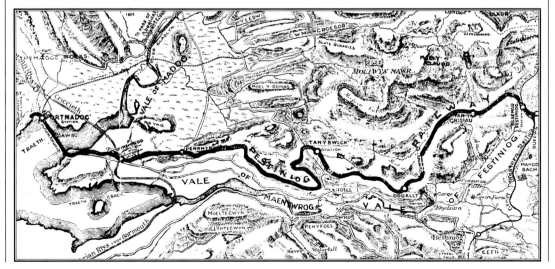

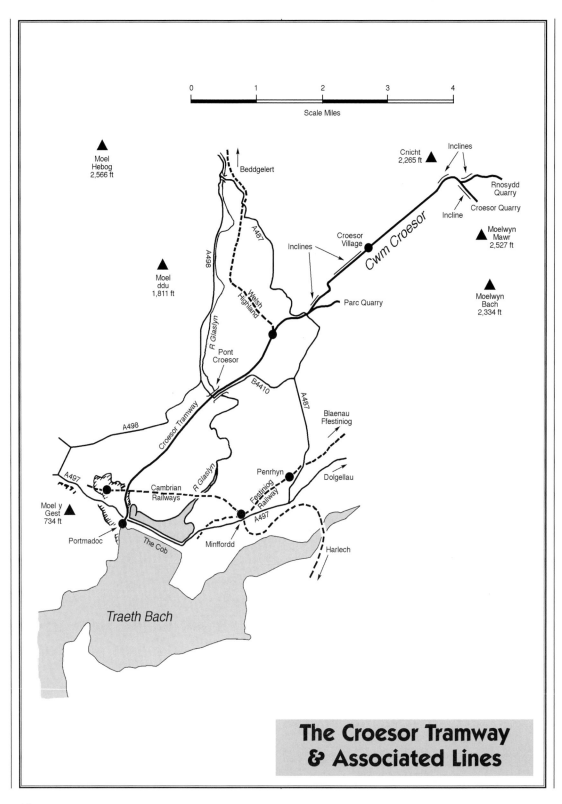

Scale Miles

Moel
Hebog
2,566 ft

Beddgelert

Cnicht
2,265 ft

Inclines

Rnosydd
Quarry

Croesor Quarry

Incline

Moelwyn
Mawr
2,527 ft

Cwm Croesor

Croesor
Village

Inclines

Moelwyn
Bach
2,334 ft

Moel
ddu
1,811 ft

Parc Quarry

Welsh
Highland

R Glaslyn

Pont
Croesor

B4410

A487

A498

A497

A498

Croesor Tramway

Blaenau
Ffestiniog

R Glaslyn

Penrhyn

Dolgellau

Cambrian
Railways

Festiniog
Railway

Moel y
Gest
734 ft

Portmadoc

The Cob

Minffordd

A497

Harlech

Traeth Bach

**The Croesor Tramway
& Associated Lines**

commences at or near the Rock called *Carrig Hylldrem* in the Parish of *Llanfrothen* and the County of *Merioneth*, and terminates at or near *Ynyscerrigduon* at *Portmadoc* in the Parish of *Ynyscynhaiarn* and County of *Carnarvon*'; a total of 4½ miles. Permission was given, subject to Board of Trade approval, for the gauge to be increased 'from Two Feet to any Gauge not exceeding Four Feet Eight Inches and a Half'. Roberts was designated one of the original directors and was allowed to be compensated by the company in respect of the tramway's construction. An extension from Porthmadog to Borth-y-Gest was also sanctioned.

For reasons that remain unclear a further 2½ miles of the 1864 tramway within the Croesor Valley, including two inclines, were not covered by the Act and remained under Roberts's control. The five company directors held all the issued share capital, yet within five years the company appeared to be in financial difficulties, for it was mortgaged for £8,000.

Below: Looking up Cwm Croesor, with the Croesor Tramway's Llanfrothen-Nantmor road level crossing in the foreground, 1947. *J. I. C. Boyd/Real Photographs*

In 1877 Spooner tried to persuade the Festiniog Railway Co to link up with the North Wales Narrow Gauge Railways' proposed Rhyd Ddu terminus. This would be achieved by taking over and re-laying part of the Croesor Tramway and by building a link line thence. He also proposed a rack railway from Rhyd Ddu to the summit of Snowdon! The Festiniog was not interested.

A second Act was obtained in 1879, authorising a three-mile extension to Beddgelert, a further £23,000 capital being authorised to pay for it; the company was allowed, if it wished, to maintain and operate the extension as a separate undertaking. The company was also allowed to enter into agreements with the Cambrian Railways and/or the Festiniog Railway for 'working, use, management and maintenance of their respective railways' and to change its name to The Portmadoc, Croesor & Beddgelert Tram Railway Company (PCBTRC). If the extension was maintained as a separate undertaking it was to be known as the Portmadoc, Croesor, & Beddgelert Tram Railway Company's Beddgelert Extension.

The impetus for this second Act, however, came from a company called The Tramways Corporation Ltd, which promoted the Croesor and

its Beddgelert extension as a railway that could match the Festiniog for traffic and dividends. The identities of the backers of the Corporation are unknown; except for Roberts, who became secretary, the CPRC directors ceased to be involved. PCBTRC shares were offered to the public shortly after the Act was obtained. Neither extension was carried out but the target of Beddgelert and sanction for Festiniog co-operation established a pattern for future developments.

The 1879 Act was only one of several attempts to get a railway to Beddgelert and not all were narrow gauge. The scheme that probably came closest to success was the standard gauge Beddgelert Railway, authorised in 1865. In Parliamentary terms the route was divided into three railways:

No 1, from a junction with the Aberystwyth & Welsh Coast Railway at Porthmadog to a point about 310yd from Gelert's Grave at Beddgelert; No 2, between the Beddgelert terminus of Railway No 1 and a point north of the Beddgelert-Capel Curig Turnpike Road; No 3, between Railway No 1 and 'the Ballast Bank on the South Side of the public Pier Wharf at *Portmadoc*, and West of the *Festiniog* Railway Station at *Portmadoc*'.

A second Beddgelert Railway Act was obtained in 1866, to authorise an extension to Llyn Gwynant and a two-mile deviation of the original route near Beddgelert. Some work was carried out on the 1865 route and may still be seen, notably the abutments for a bridge crossing a Glaslyn tributary near Nantmor. Getting this route through the Aberglaslyn Pass would have incurred considerable expense. The Beddgelert Siding, later known by Col Stephens as the Gelert Siding, appears to have been part of the Beddgelert Railway although it is not shown on the deposited plans retained in the County Archives at Caernarfon.

This attempt was followed by that of the North Wales Narrow Gauge Railways (NWNGR). In its 1872 Act approval was gained for a 22-mile line, commencing 'by a junction with the Croesor and Portmadoc Railway' and terminating at Betws-y-coed, the NWNGR's General Undertaking, and for powers to work the Croesor line. In supporting, and being a promoter of, this scheme Roberts

Below: The same location, looking in the opposite direction, towards Porthmadog, in 1951. On the right a wagon has been abandoned. *W. Bareham*

agreed to make the relevant section of the Croesor & Portmadoc Railway fit for NWNGR trains, but only when half the NWNGR General Undertaking had been built. He was an objector to the Beddgelert Railway.

In 1882 the Croesor company established a further link to the NWNGR when a second mortgage was obtained, this time from the receiver for that line, James Cholmeley Russell, in the sum of £330. At the same time the company was placed in receivership by the first mortgage lender. The sum of the two mortgages, £8,330, matched the maximum amount authorised to be borrowed on mortgage by the 1865 Act.

Attempts were still being made to get the FR interested in the Croesor and its Beddgelert extension, with Roberts himself offering in 1882 to hand over an extended Croesor to the FR in exchange for FR shares.

In 1901 the Portmadoc, Croesor & Beddgelert Tram Railway Company's assets and powers were sold to the newly established Portmadoc, Beddgelert & South Snowdon Railway Co (PBSSR) for £10,000, pursuant to the PBSSR's 1901 Act. The PCBTRC was still in receivership, the two mortgages remaining outstanding and seriously in arrears. Russell accepted his £330 in full settlement of capital and interest, ending his involvement with the undertaking. Notwithstanding, Hugh Beaver Roberts came out owning all the PCBTRC's share capital. The Act's preamble stated that the passenger-carrying powers had never been implemented and that its state of repair was 'not such as to justify or allow the conveyance of passengers thereon'. The Act dissolved the PCBTRC on completion of the sale.

Despite these changes in ownership and attempts to build the Croesor Tramway into a much larger undertaking, the tramway continued as it always had done. In the later years of the 19th century, traffic was sometimes sufficient to justify the employment of four men on haulage. The busiest section was between Porthmadog harbour and the Beddgelert siding, including carriage of slate from the Festiniog Railway before the exchange yard was built at Minffordd in 1872, and afterwards when Minffordd was too busy. The following description is extracted from Major

Below: Cnicht is prominent in this view of Croesor Junction looking towards Cwm Croesor. The WHR ran off to the left and the Croesor Tramway straight on. The pylons are those of the North Wales Power & Traction Co. *Real Photographs*

G. C. Spring's report commissioned by the Festiniog Railway in 1921:

Croesor Branch

139. The Croesor branch line takes off the Portmadoc Wharf lines, and skirts reclaimed estuary land, crossing the Cambrian Railway [sic] about half a mile from Portmadoc Station.

    A number of slate loading and wharf sidings are thrown off, paralleling the Cambrian Railway slate loading docks.

140. The crossing of the Cambrian line is on the level and approximately a square crossing and is controlled by a signal cabin in charge of the Cambrian Railway with trapped points on each side set in the narrow gauge line.

141. No locomotive has been over the branch for a very considerable period and the Permanent Way is for the most part in a state of disrepair. It is railed for the first mile with flangeless quarry siding type of rail, about 21lb per yard seated on CI Chairs.

    The majority of the sleepers for this distance are rotten and at least 20% require renewal before a locomotive of the shunting engine type (Welsh Pony Class) can be run over without constant risk of derailment and damage to the engines. All the points and crossings which are of the short lead tramway type should also be replaced before an engine can be passed over them.

142. There is no telegraph but a telephone line is in working existence from the Park Quarry Office 5 miles from Portmadoc to the site of the Cambrian Wharf Siding.

143. A loading platform and siding about 200 yards from Portmadoc Station serves a flour mill.

144. From 1 mile approximately to the Junction with the partly constructed Beddgelert Railway, a good 30ft Steel rail with 11 creosoted sleepers per rail length is laid, the rail being flat footed and weighing about 30 to 35lb per yard. Bearing plates are fixed at joint sleepers.

145. This portion of the permanent way is in excellent condition, except for a number of the sleepers which have been damaged between the rail bearings by horses' feet.

146. The ballast is thin but good, being granite chippings.

147. There is only one major bridge, consisting of (8) 25ft wooden girder spans on slate rubble piers over the Glaslyn River.

The girders are rail bearers have [sic] longitudinal sleepers directly over them and a 4in timber decking.

    The piers are decidedly faulty, having been damaged by flood water and require repointing.

148. The wooden girders should be strong enough to take the shunting engine at 5 miles per hour but the piers should be examined and repaired where necessary.

149. It is understood that the County Council have the question of reconstruction of this bridge under consideration and the Railway connection should not be overlooked.

150. The Park Quarries at Croesor appear to be very thoroughly equipped with machinery and power and are said to be in process of considerable expansion.

151. The present tonnage of slates sent from Croesor (Park) Quarries is from 80 to 100 tons per month. This all proceeds to the Cambrian Railway sidings about 1 mile from Portmadoc Station and is at present horse drawn. The output from these Quarries is said to be increasing and it is said that the pre-war monthly output was 300 tons.

Change came only when the Welsh Highland Railway was built in 1922, when about three miles of the route was relaid to support locomotive traction. Such traffic that the quarries still generated was usually exchanged at the newly created Croesor Junction, although at busier times a locomotive was sent from Porthmadog to fetch it.

Roberts's part of the tramway, the non-parliamentary section in the valley itself, was offered for sale at auction in 1936, without finding a buyer. Following pressure from the local authorities the entire Croesor route was left in situ when the remaining Welsh Highland Railway track materials were lifted in 1941. The authorities were concerned that the Croesor quarries would not be able to reopen after the war if there was no railway as there was no road alternative in the valley. Rails on the lower section were lifted in 1948/9 and the remainder in the 1950s.

The Croesor Tramway has never been formally closed.

Right: An unusually long passenger train, newly arrived at Dinas c1890. One of the Cleminson six-wheeled brakes is coupled next to the locomotive. *Real Photographs*

The North Wales Narrow Gauge Railways

The next strand to come into the Welsh Highland Railway story is that of the North Wales Narrow Gauge Railways (NWNGR). This is arguably Charles Easton Spooner's greatest contribution. His motivation was probably twofold. He owned a slate quarry that came to be served by the Bryngwyn branch and was probably trying to maintain a narrow gauge monopoly on slate traffic in the face of competition from the LNWR. Or perhaps Spooner was attempting to create something out of nothing that would appear to be of such value to the LNWR that he would be bought out at a substantial price. The Euston-based company's acquisition of the Carnarvonshire Railway and its running powers into Porthmadog in 1870, and the operation of the 'Welshman' express from Euston to Porthmadog via Afon Wen, could well have come about in response to Spooner's politicking.

Parliament responded to it by severely clipping his wings. Proposals for eight railways were submitted. The objectives were:

To link Porthmadog with Corwen, using part of the Croesor & Portmadoc Railway, and then via Beddgelert, Capel Curig and Betws-y-coed (Railways Nos 1-3);
A branch to the LNWR station at Betws-y-coed (No 4);
A branch to Penmachno from Railway No 2 (No 5);
A branch from the LNWR (Carnarvonshire Railway) near Llanwnda to a 'point about four chains and fifty links measured in an easterly direction from the south-east corner of the

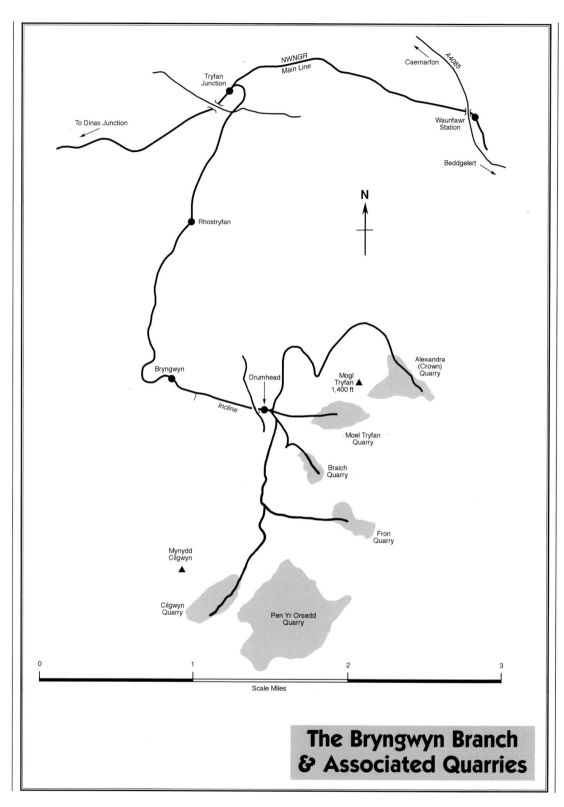

The Bryngwyn Branch
& Associated Quarries

farmhouse called Vron Haulog', Bryngwyn (No 6);

A branch from Railway No 6 to 'a field called Cae Mawr on Ffridd Isaf Farm', Rhyd Ddu (No 7);

A branch from Pwllheli to Porthdinllaen (No 8).

Of these, only Railways 1, 6 and 7 gained approval, in 1872. Railway No 1, (from the Croesor & Portmadoc Railway to Betws-y-coed) was defined as the General Undertaking and Railways Nos 6 and 7 as the Moel Tryfan Undertaking. The former was to be capitalised at

Below: This map was one of several published by the NWNGR in support of its Parliamentary ambitions, although this version does not include Railway No 4, at Betws-y-coed, or Railway No 8, Pwllheli-Porthdinllaen. The original map is coloured — the General Undertaking runs from Porthmadog to Corwen, the Moel Tryfan Undertaking from Llanwnda. *Peter Johnson Collection*

£150,000; the latter at £66,000. The respective capital sums and accounts were to be kept separately.

The Act identified the promoters as including Livingston Thompson (a director of the Festiniog Railway) and Hugh Beaver Roberts, previously encountered. It defined the gauge as 'two feet'; it could be increased at any time (not exceeding 4ft 8½in) subject to receiving Board of Trade approval.

The company decided to start with the Moel Tryfan Undertaking. As three early directors and the company's engineer owned quarries in the Bryngwyn area, nothing more need be said to explain this preference. First a contract was let for its construction on 23 December 1872, then the company issued a prospectus and on 23 April 1873 it entered into an agreement with Roberts, whereby he undertook to operate the railway for 21 years on lease. The North Wales Narrow Gauge Railways (Lease) Act 1873 confirmed this arrangement. The company clearly thought it was on to a good thing with it. Roberts was expected

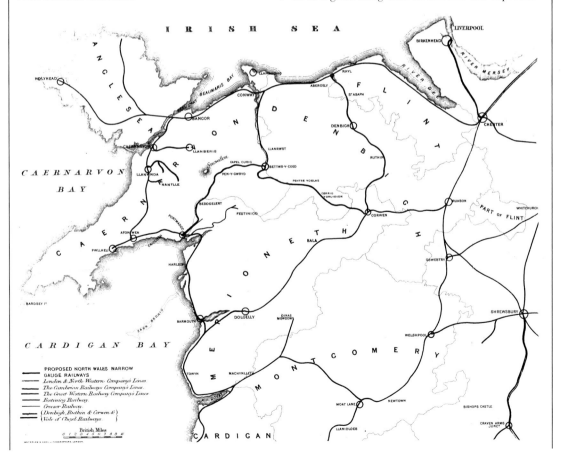

Above: A train, consisting of two different brake composites, about to leave Rhyd Ddu for Dinas. *F. Moore/WHR(P)*

Left: Rhyd Ddu was equipped with a splendid range of buildings, seen here after the station was renamed Snowdon in 1893. Refreshments were provided from the wooden building at the right of the range. The gent leaning on the telegraph post has adopted the stance often taken by late 20th century mobile phone users! *Gwyn Price Collection*

Below left: Bryngwyn, looking towards the incline and the quarries, in NWNGR days. The goods shed's shadow falls on the right. *WHR(P)*

Right: The NWNGR on its last legs. *Russell* with one of the occasional goods trains at Waunfawr in 1920. *C. R. Clinker/Real Photographs*

to cover the debenture interest at 6%, the company's administrative expenses, 6% dividend on share capital and a proportion of any profits made additional to the total of those sums.

Another of the remarkable features of the agreement was the requirement that Roberts should 'have all the locomotives (except shunting engines) in use on the demised premises constructed and maintained according to the principle known as 'Fairlie's Patents', and shall pay the royalty of £300 per engine'. Roberts was allocated £10,000 by the company for the purchase of locomotives and rolling stock. The stock was to be returned to the company on expiry of the lease, or on determination if sooner, to the full £10,000 value. That is, with no recognition being made of depreciation or wear and tear.

Construction was started in May 1873, with completion of both lines being anticipated within 12 months. There appears to have been a lack of communication between railway and contractor, with the contractor losing interest and slowing down work as payments from the company got in arrears, although the contractor had received £40,000 of the contracted £56,000.

In 1874 work ceased and the contractor started to remove track materials he had bought. The company took the contractor to arbitration, expecting to win, but the arbitrator found against it. Unsettled by the delays, and probably taking time to ponder upon the wisdom of the contract he had signed, Roberts repudiated his lease. The company did not recognise his right to do so but pragmatically accepted that it was unable to deal with him from a position of strength.

Little progress was made by the contractor, who succeeded with a further arbitration award against the company, and in August 1876 the appointment of a new contractor was announced. By an Act of 1876 the company abandoned its General Undertaking and gained approval for further fund-raising. Declaring that the Moel Tryfan Undertaking's £66,000 capital and a further £22,000 borrowed on mortgage had all been spent, the company gained approval to raise an additional £40,000 in ordinary or preferential shares, or both.

The new contractor made good progress and the line to Bryngwyn was brought into use for goods and mineral traffic during 1877. On the line to Rhyd Ddu the track had reached Quellyn Lake and was being used for goods services. Following inspections by the Board of Trade, both lines were approved for passenger traffic, to Rhostryfan on the Bryngwyn branch, from 28 January 1878. Five months later the main line was extended to Snowdon Ranger, a distance of nearly a mile further, and approval gained for passenger use. It was to be 1881 before the line to Rhyd Ddu was opened to traffic.

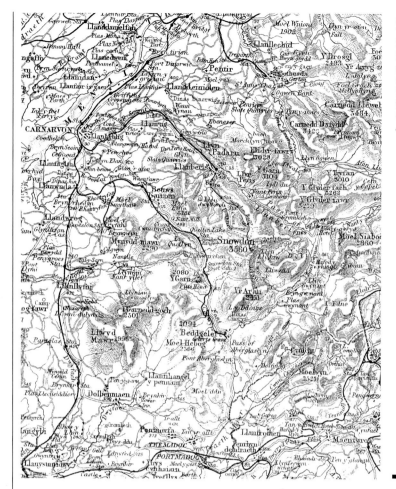

Left:
This map of Snowdonia shows the route of the NWNGR's Beddgelert extension, apparently with its terminus adjacent to Gelert's grave instead of 'twenty yards or thereabouts east of the reservoir of the Goat Hotel'. *Peter Johnson Collection*

These 12 miles completed the NWNGR's Moel Tryfan Undertaking. Despite all its earlier, and later, ambitions nothing more was achieved by the railway. When route expansion did come, the Moel Tryfan Undertaking was substantially moribund and the impetus came from elsewhere. The main line to Rhyd Ddu was nine miles long, the branch to Bryngwyn Drumhead, the top of the incline, three miles, starting from Tryfan Junction, two miles from Llanwnda. At the latter a joint station was established with the LNWR and named Dinas Junction, the LNWR's Llanwnda station continuing in use with that name. When times were good the main traffic was slate from the Bryngwyn quarries bound for Caernarfon, carried at the cost of transhipment at Dinas Junction for the short onward journey to the port.

Quite why the more populous Beddgelert, 3½ miles from Rhyd Ddu, was never targeted at this stage, to make the obvious link with the General

Undertaking, is not known. Even if the gradients needed to get into the village were off-putting, a terminus near Pitt's Head, 'Beddgelert Road', would have made some sense. As it was, the railway benefited from a mix of passenger, agricultural and mineral traffic, although, as will be seen, not in any substantial amount. Rhyd Ddu station's location by the start of the shortest walking route to Snowdon's summit was to bring tourists to the line, and horse-drawn road vehicles provided the link to Beddgelert, the connections being included in the railway's timetable.

Despite Roberts having held his lease for only a year, and then some three years before the railway was sufficiently complete for trains to be run, his brief tenure still had an impact on the railway's future. He had ordered the manufacture of locomotives and rolling stock for the line. The company itself took over orders for carriages and wagons, paying for them by instalments. Another solution was found for the locomotives, presumably because the company had insufficient resources to fund them directly.

The Moel Tryfan Rolling Stock Co Ltd (MTRSC) was established in December 1878 to 'purchase...the locomotives...and rolling stock now in use by the NWNG Railways Co'; seven partners, including James Cholmeley Russell, had capitalised it to the sum of £10,000. It appears that Russell had completed the purchase of at least the 1875-built locomotives and some other rolling stock, instead of Roberts, and had been hiring it to the company. He sold it to MTRSC for £3,630. Russell was owed nearly £1,000 by the company in respect of hiring fees and that debt was assigned to MTRSC also. MTRSC promptly sued for the arrears and succeeded in putting the company into receivership, with Russell appointed as receiver.

Russell was to influence the fortunes, or otherwise, of the NWNGR until his death in 1911 but the NWNGR was not his only railway interest. In 1880 he was manager of the Manchester & Milford Railway and was later one of the promoters of the Vale of Rheidol Railway. He became NWNGR chairman in 1879.

Having got the railway operating, the financial position did not improve as it might have done, for the slate trade, on which so much depended, was in a state of depression. The loss of the main market at a time critical to a railway's performance will be encountered again before the end of this book.

In 1880 a debenture issue totalling £50,000 was approved to eliminate the company's debt and to acquire the locomotives and rolling stock from MTRSC. MTRSC was wound up in 1889 and dissolved in 1894. £39,593 of the debentures had been issued by 1990; the NWNGR remained in receivership.

Traffic had improved by 1882, when Russell was reporting good, increasing, business in the carriage of slate, coal and lime. On the passenger side, a decline in third class passengers was accompanied by an increase in those travelling first and second. Extra trains ran on Saturdays but the railway never ran on Sundays. The railway had a bad record for reportable incidents, both derailments and collisions. In two cases, in 1878 and 1901, staff members were killed.

Despite its debts, the NWNGR was soon returning to Parliament, in 1885 obtaining the North Wales Narrow Gauge Railways (Extensions, &c) Act. This provided for a deviation of the Bryngwyn incline and an extension from Dinas to Caernarfon. The incline was 'owing to its severe gradients and formation and the method of working it capable of being used only for goods and mineral traffic and it is in that and other respects inadequate to meet the requirements of and unsuitable for the district'. The Caernarfon extension was designed to avoid the break of gauge at Dinas; the line would have terminated opposite the castle, 'near the boat-house in the occupation of the Carnarvon Rowing Club'. Where the line passed under the LNWR the NWNGR was to provide a wrought-iron girder bridge not less than 25ft in width between the parapets. The company also had power to complete agreements with the borough of Caernarfon and/or the Caernarfon Harbour Trust for bridging the Afon Seiont, presumably by the terminus, and to purchase the river ferry that the bridge would supersede. The owner of the Coed Helen estate obtained a protective clause requiring that 'the elevation of any stations...shall be of such reasonable ornamental character as the owner shall require'. The use of Crown Lands at the incline summit was permitted by a 998-year lease, annual rental of £5 being payable — the Official Receiver was still paying this rent on behalf of the Welsh Highland Railway (Light Railway) Company, in receivership, as this book was being written in 1998.

In recognition of the receiver's interest in the NWNGR these extensions were to be maintained as a separate undertaking, distinct and apart from the Moel Tryfan Undertaking, to be known as the Carnarvon and Bryngwyn Extensions Undertaking. This undertaking was to be capitalised at £28,000, with powers to borrow further sums on mortgage.

No action was taken either to raise the funding or to build either of these lines. In 1890 another Act granted an extension of time. The Act also sanctioned the issuing of £10,000 in debentures. These would redeem £6,000 existing debentures and pay for continuous brakes, additional rolling stock, a telegraph/telephone system, turntables, additional buildings, sheds, signals and 'other matters and things for the permanent improvement of the Moel Tryfan Undertaking...'. Installation of Westinghouse brakes was completed by 1894, at which time the last of eight new carriages funded by the 1890 debentures was delivered. There were never any turntables on the NWNGR.

In 1900 the railway obtained the North Wales Narrow Gauge Railways (Beddgelert Light Railway Extension) Order under the auspices of the 1896 Light Railways Act. This was obtained in response to attempts being made by outsiders to fill the gap between Rhyd Ddu and the Croesor Tramway, and thence to Porthmadog. The NWNGR line was to be four miles long, terminating 'twenty yards or thereabouts east of the reservoir of the Goat Hotel'. Once again the extension was to be a separate undertaking, 'the Extension Undertaking' no less, and all capital and accounts were to be kept separately. The authorised capital was £13,800, with approval given for mortgage borrowing of £4,600. The Order specified that rails should weigh at least 41½ lb per yard and that check rails should be used on curves of less than three chains radius. It was extremely detailed on the fixings to be used on flat-bottom rail. While the Order was being processed, the Board of Trade was exercised about the implications of the line having 1 in 40 gradients. They would be too steep, said the Board, if the company decided to take advantage of the proposed power to increase the gauge up to standard gauge. The company agreed to withdrawal of the relevant clause, on the understanding that fresh powers could be obtained if needed. The Board of Trade apparently failed to appreciate that a standard gauge line on the same alignment would have impossibly tight curves!

On 16 April 1901 the company called a special general meeting to pass the special resolutions necessary to bring the Extension Undertaking into effect. A little work was done to the south of Rhyd Ddu and around Pitt's Head, and in 1906 the powers were revived and transferred to the Portmadoc, Beddgelert & South Snowdon Railway (PBSSR) by means of a Light Railway Order. An agreement made between the NWNGR, the PBSSR and the North Wales Power & Traction Co 'containing the bases of working arrangements between the companies and the construction of railways' was approved by NWNGR shareholders at a special meeting held in November 1904. An account of PBSSR activities follows in the next chapter.

In 1903 the railway's reputation for accidents continued with two passenger train derailments, one causing injury to a staff member. The only incident considered worthy of reporting in the *Railway Times* was a 'serious landslip' near Rhostryfan, on the Bryngwyn branch, that had blocked the line and caused traffic to be suspended.

The NWNGR returned to the Light Railway Commissioners in November 1903, seeking a

further Order 'authorising the working and maintenance of the Moel Tryfan Undertaking of the North Wales Narrow Gauge Railways Company as a Light Railway and other matters'. The Order, made in 1905, authorised that the NWNGR could be worked as a light railway; that it could be worked by electrical power; and lease itself to the PBSSR and enter into operating and maintenance agreements with the PBSSR. It could issue £12,000 (maximum) debentures and rank some existing debentures behind the 1905 issue in priority for interest payments. The Order contained two provisos that appear to demonstrate a lack of confidence in the likely continued success of the venture. Firstly, relating to the power to lease to the PBSSR, 'every such lease shall imply a condition of re-entry if the lessees discontinue the working of the railway... for the space of three months (such discontinuance not being occasioned by circumstances beyond the reasonable control of the lessees *for which purpose the want of sufficient funds shall not be considered a circumstance beyond their reasonable control*)' — author's italics! Secondly, £2,000 of the 1905 debentures was prescribed for the purposes of the appointment of a receiver!

All these powers and provisos did no good for the NWNGR, however, for it was already in decline; not that it had ever achieved great success. In fact it only kept going because the PB&SSR funded the order for a new locomotive, Hunslet 2-6-2T *Russell* in 1906. Two years later the funds were found for another Fairlie, 0-6-4T *Gowrie*. In 1912 the railway was actually making sufficient profit to enable debenture interest to be paid — an exceptional situation in its history. Notwithstanding this improvement, the Bryngwyn passenger service was withdrawn from 1 January 1914 and all main line services followed from 1 November 1916. A report published in *Railway & Travel Monthly* in 1917 described the railway at this time; everything was run-down and holes seen in the panelling of carriages. The writer commented, 'A motor bus service along a road which follows the line bids fair to prove the proverbial 'last straw'.' After 1916 only the Bryngwyn branch goods service was operated — very likely the main objective of the NWNGR's promoters in the 19th century.

In 1921, with the Welsh Highland Railway in prospect, the Festiniog Railway commissioned Major Spring to report on its component parts, as already mentioned in Chapter 2. On the NWNGR he reported as follows:

Continued on page 29

NWNGR Scenes

Right: Beddgelert leading one of the Vulcan Fairlies on a long train at Dinas, c1892. The first three coaches are four-wheelers. *A. G. Symons/ WHR(P)*

Centre right: A Dinas-bound train at Rhyd Ddu forms a backdrop for a family scene, with the males on the footplate and the ladies waiting patiently alongside the train. The coal in the bunker will need some attention from the fireman before it gets into the locomotive's firebox. *Peacock/Gwyn Price Collection*

Below: A typical NWNGR scene attracted the attention of the postcard photographer. *Gwyn Price Collection*

Above: The railway at Plas-y-nant, with Quellyn Lake in the background. *Photochrom/Gwyn Price Collection*

Left: Moel Tryfan and what appears to be a lightly loaded or empty train at Plas-y-nant. The coaches are on one of the NWNGR's characteristic bowstring bridges. *WHR(P)*

Below left: Snowdon Ranger lies at the other end of Quellyn Lake, seen in the railway's later days. *WHR(P)*

Above right: One of the single Fairlies at Tryfan Junction with a (very) short mixed train. *Paul Ingham Collection*

The North Wales Narrow Gauge Railway

General
1. This railway (23½ gauge) is constructed from Dinas Junction (L&NWRly) to Tryfan Junction (mile 3) and thence to Rhyddu [sic] or Snowdon Station a distance of 9½ miles. From Tryfan Junction (mile 3) a branch runs to Bryngwyn (4¼ miles) and thence over a 1 in 10 incline operated by rope haulage to Drumhead (6¼ miles)

Traffic
2. The Railway has been closed for some years to passenger traffic. The following goods and mineral tonnage was carried in July and August, 1921:

	Jul 1921	*Aug 1921*
Slates from Bryngwyn	411 tons	663 tons
Coal	178 tons	353 tons
Forwarded Goods	10 tons	24 tons
Timber	6 tons	
TOTAL	605 tons	1,040 tons

3. The whole of the tonnage with the exception of a small coal traffic originates from the Bryngwyn Quarries for transport to Dinas Junction where the slates are transhipped by the Narrow Gauge Staff into NWRly wagons at an inclusive rate.

Staff
4. The Staff is controlled by a Traffic Superintendent and work is limited to four days a week only, the staff consists of the following:

Traffic Superintendent	1
Clerk (female) Dinas Junction	1
Clerk (female) Snowdon Station	1
Transhippers [sic]	5
Foreman	1
Permanent Way men	2
Carpenter & Wagon Fettler	1
Blacksmith & Wagon Fettler	1
Striker	1
Fitter	1
Driver	1
Fireman	1
Guard Brakesman	1
Inclined ropeway brakesman at Bryngwyn	1
TOTAL	19

The cost of the Staff per fortnight is £84 in wages and salaries.

The Traffic Superintendent controls the working of the Railway and in addition performs the duty of Station-master for the L&NW Station at Dinas Junction.

Rolling Stock
5. There *are two* locomotives.

1. *Moel Tryfan* 6 wheeled coupled tank about 46 years old, by the 'Vulcan', rebuilt 1903, reboilered and retubed 1912.
2. *Russell* 6 wheeled coupled tank with single pony at each end built 1906 by the 'Hunslet' both engines appeared to be in good order.

The former can draw 4 and the latter 9 composite coaches (50 passengers each) up the steepest gradient on the line.

Coaching Stock

6. The Coaching stock has long been out of use, and is much deteriorated through lack of paint.

Composite Carriages	11
4 Wheel Brake Vans	1
Brake Van & Passenger (comp)	2
All Westinghouse fitted	

Goods Stock

7. Slate wagons tare from 15cwt to 22cwt

load 2 tons	90
Open goods Wagons load 2 tons	12
Coal Wagons	13
Bolster Wagons	14
Bolster check Wagons	20

Telegraph

8. The telegraph is not in working order, two wires and posts are standing throughout. The telephone is in operation from Snowdon Station to Dinas Junction with one connection to Waun-fawr Station.

Signalling

9. The Railway was fitted when passenger service was in operation with block instruments throughout, and Staff and Ticket Boxes, Tryfan Jn and Waun-fawr are crossing stations and provided with loop lines. [sic!]

Stations

9. The following are the Stations:

Main

Dinas Junction	Mile 0
Tryfan Junction	Mile 3
Waun-fawr	Mile 4
Betws Garmon	Mile 5
Quellyn Lake	Mile 7½
Snowdon Station	Mile 9½

Branch to Bryngwyn

Tryfan Junction	Mile 3
Rhos Tryfan	Mile 3¾
Bryngwyn	Mile 5½
Drumhead	Mile 6½

Terminal Facilities

10. Terminal facilities at Dinas include the following:

Office and Station Building
Station Master's House
Parcels Office
Booking Office
Waiting Room
Warehouse and tranship shed with 30cwt dock crane
Engine Shed Running
Blacksmithy
Coaching Vehicle Shed and Carpenters Shop
Oil Stores and Coal Stores Shed
Platelayers Tool Hut
Engine Water Tank
Signal Cabin with facing points interlocked to signals
Coal tilting table from NWRly to Narrow Gauge
Timber Tranship Stage

Train Service

11. One train only per day is run 4 days per week to Bryngwyn to feed the slate quarries with empties and to remove and haul the rail wagons to Dinas Junction. When necessary a trip to Snowdon Station is run with coals or smalls.

12. The Staff employed at Dinas Junction does not appear excessive, but it appears wrong to employ a foreman and four men on tranship work on a daily wage. This work *should certainly be placed on contract*.

Permanent Way Maintenance

13. The two permanent way men cannot of course keep the Permanent Way even weeded and the track is in a very poor state of maintenance. Between Dinas Junction and Bryngwyn Station the majority of the traffic takes place and 1,000 sleepers have been recently renewed in this length, and the [sic] bars introduced to check the spreading of the gauge. A further 500 sleepers are urgently required. Bryngwyn Station Yard requires immediate attention.

14. The track from Tryfan (mile 3) to about a mile from Snowdon Station say 8½ mile requires at least 300 new sleepers per mile, before any passenger trains could be run without serious risk of derailment.

Every curve requires packing and lifting and a lot of ballast especially under joint sleepers is required.

From Mile 8½ to Snowdon Station ie the 92 foot span bridge onwards the track is well ballast [sic] and in good order as regards sleepers.

Fencing

15. Fencing is much broken down, new standards being required everywhere. Stone boundary walls likewise require rebuilding.

Bridges

16. With the exception of the longitudinal sleepers on the girder bridges, both arched masonry and girder bridges appear to be in good order.

Signalling

17. The crossing and terminal stations are provided with signal cabins and Lever Frames at each. These cabins are of timber and completely rotted. Distant, Home and Starter signals are provided and signal posts are very dilapidated and the semaphore gear useless. In the event of re-opening the line to passenger traffic the signal cabin at Dinas Junction should not be perpetuated. A ground frame with distant repeater placed just outside the station home operated by the Station Master will answer the purpose.

Loco & Rolling Stock Repairs

18. All Light repairs to Locos and rolling stock are carried out by the Staff enumerated in para 4. Heavy repairs to locos are when necessary done under contract. There are no Machinery [sic] or Lathes in the loco running shed.

Route

19. From the passenger point of view the route from Dinas Junction to Snowdon Station (Rhyddu) connects points of no particular importance whilst the route from Dinas Junction to Bryngwyn is similarly prejudiced.
20. The Railway route from Dinas to Bryngwyn is fairly well populated and includes at the Bryngwyn end some large Quarry Villages, such as Carmel, population 700, Cesarea population 400, and a number of small agricultural holdings.
21. The Permanent Way consists of 41 UPP Steel Rail on 11 sleepers per 30ft length, dog spiked with 4 holed fish plates. The sharp curves and steep ruling gradient cause trouble at the station yards owing to the travel of the rail down the grade.

At Bryngwyn Station Yard the points and crossings are unfit to carry a locomotive.

Bryngwyn Incline

22. The incline to the Amalgamated Quarries is about ½ mile and about 1 in 10 slope. The Railway Company's Staff here, contrary to general practice, work the wagons over the incline. The Amalgamated Quarry Company work the following quarries at the head of the incline. Alexander, Moel Tryfan, Bryaich [sic], Cilcwyn [sic], and about to open a further at Vron.
23. Owing to the weak rope used on the incline it is possible to lower three wagons only at a time, so that 3 to 4 hours are occupied in handling a train of 20 wagons over this incline. The Amalgamated Quarries appear likely to extend their output considerably in the near future and it would appear possible to eliminate this incline by a method of adhesion back shunts, connecting the station at Bryngwyn with the Quarry Sidings at Drumhead.
24. Should this alteration be done, it is more than probable that the slate traffic from the large Penyrorsedd Quarries employing some 800 hands would be diverted from the present day horse drawn tramway outlet at Nantille [sic] over the North Wales Narrow Gauge to Dinas Junction.
25. As noted before Dinas Junction forms no real objective for passenger traffic, but it is considered that were the line between Dinas Junction and Carnarvon to be connected a paying passenger traffic could be instituted between Bryngwyn and Carnarvon.
26. To avoid expensive staff, the shuttle trains on the punch ticket system could be run and signalling obviated. This appears to have been exceedingly elaborated. Tryfan Junction has no less than 10 Signals and a cabin of 20 lever [sic]
27. As long however as the railway journey entails a change at Dinas Junction, the passenger traffic will continue to utilise the Motor Bus Service which now plies between Bryngwyn and Carnarvon, with an hourly service on Saturday afternoon, the Quarry men's half holiday.
28. Cesarea, Carmel, Rhos, Tryfan and Waunfawr are large and well populated villages, whose only trade and shopping centre is Carnarvon.

Continued on page 36

NWNGR Locomotives

Above: This attractive portrait shows *Snowdon Ranger* standing outside Dinas loco shed. The loco received a heavy overhaul, including a new boiler, at the hands of Davies & Metcalfe in 1902. In 1917 its frames were used to rebuild *Moel Tryfan* and the remainder was scrapped.
Real Photographs

Left: Moel Tryfan, also built by Vulcan Foundry Ltd in 1875, is seen at Dinas in 1909. Here its tank side appears to have been in the wars.
Real Photographs

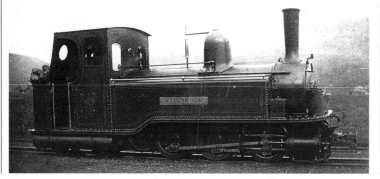

Lower left: The various buckets and boxes carried on the front footplate of NWNGR locomotives contained supplementary sand supplies, as seen here on *Moel Tryfan*. In 1903 *Moel Tryfan* followed *Snowdon Ranger* to Davies & Metcalfe for overhaul.
Adrian Gray Collection

Above: Moel Tryfan at Rhyd Ddu sporting a magnificent headlamp on 10 September 1894. The locomotive's chimney top has received some form of modification. Rebuilt with *Snowdon Ranger's* frames in 1917, *Moel Tryfan* went on to become part of the WHR fleet from 1922. *W. G. Rear Collection*

Below: Hunslet delivered 0-6-4ST *Beddgelert* in 1878; this is the works photograph. More powerful than the Fairlies, it was ideally suited to heavy freight trains, although few photographs survive of it performing any type of duty. *Real Photographs*

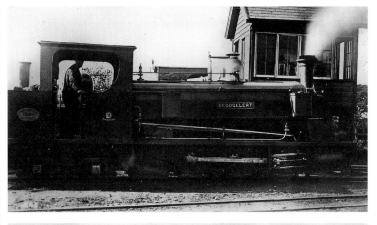

Left: Seen in Dinas loco shed yard c1905, *Beddgelert's* chimney has been replaced or shortened. The cab-side device has also been changed. *Beddgelert* was withdrawn in 1906, probably worn out. *Real Photographs*

Centre left: Beddgelert's replacement was 0-6-4T *Gowrie,* another single Fairlie, delivered by Hunslet in 1908. The loco was unnamed when first run. *Hunslet/WHR(P)*

Below: A contrasting view of *Gowrie* in traffic. This is not the only photograph of *Gowrie* running bunker-first with a lamp still on the smokebox. *Paul Ingham Collection*

Above right: A portrait of *Gowrie* ready to leave Dinas with a goods train, c1911. *Gowrie* was sold in 1915. *G. M. Perkins/ Adrian Gray Collection*

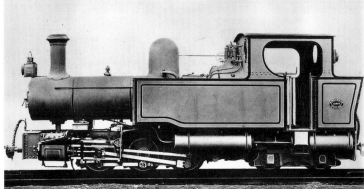

Above: Although the PBSSR bought 2-6-2T *Russell* in 1906, it was never used by that railway, being delivered to the NWNGR. The boiler-top sandbox did not survive long in service. Seen here in 1909, *Russell* appears to have been pulled out of Dinas loco shed for photography by the still unnamed *Gowrie*.
Real Photographs

Tryfan Junction to Snowdon Station

29. As stated there is little traffic over this section and the Permanent Way is in bad order, owing to the rotting sleepers. There is a probability of an increased mineral traffic from the Garrhog Quarry, between Waunfawr and Betws Garmon, the Victoria Slate Quarry (Hafod-y-Wern) near Betws Garmon Station, the Glan-r-afon [sic] Quarry near Quellyn Lake and the Cader Lake Quarry. All of which show signs of resuscitation.

Passenger Traffic

30. There is nowadays no passenger traffic at all, but should the extension to Carnarvon be constructed, a large Summer of Tourist traffic could certainly be developed.

31. The Valley of the Gwyr Fai Afon which the Railway traverses, Quellyn and Cader Lakes, the towering masses of Snowdon and Yr Arran, the very heart of Snowdonia, provide a scenic attraction that cannot be surpassed.

32. A Shuttle service from Carnarvon to Rhyddu and back would be cheap in running costs and would, it is considered, be a lucrative undertaking.

33. The service would of course fall into competition with the existing motor charabanc service, since the Carnarvon Beddgelert Road parallels the railway from Waunfawr onwards.

34. The Shuttle Service would provide a fare at about 2d per mile, a price with which the charabancs could not compete, and the

Above: In 1917 *Russell* posed at Dinas with the experimental Dick Kerr petrol-electric locomotive. *Peter Johnson Collection*

railway trip would abstract the large multitude who cannot afford charabanc fares.

35. A tourist traffic was of course in existence between Dinas Junction and Rhyddu (Snowdon Station) some years ago but it was not run as a Shuttle service nor was it of course subject to the competition of the Motor charabanc.

36. It would be worth while to get the Permanent way into Order by the renewal of the necessary sleepers and the packing of the line, before the 1922 Tourist Season. The change of trains at Dinas Junction will of course prejudice the numbers travelling to a large extent, but if suitably advertised and worked as a Shuttle Service only, the trip should attract a sufficient number to repay expenses, cost of renewals and repairs, and lay the foundation of an extended service.

37. The Railway from Rhyddu (Snowdon Station) via Beddgelert and the Aberglaslyn Pass, to the Junction with the Croesor Branch is as yet incomplete, the cuttings and formation of embankments have been completed, but bridges are ungirdered, and a tunnel remains to be pierced.

38. Steel Rails of 41lb section have been laid for a distance of 1 mile between Snowdon Station

and Beddgelert and have been utilised recently for Timber logging purposes.

39. The cost of completing the Railway from Rhyddu to Croesor Jct has already been separately estimated.

40. The completion of the above section and the Dinas Junction Carnarvon section would enable through service to be run from Carnarvon to Blaenau Festiniog.

41. There is little resident population either in the Aberglaslyn Valley or at Beddgelert, but a very large tourist traffic traverses the route during four months of the year.

42. The service of Motor charabancs parallel the railway practically the whole distance, but since they carry neither luggage nor goods, and their rates for passenger traffic would be higher than those charged by the Railway, the competition is not as severe as would appear at first sight.

42a. There does not appear much likelihood of a mineral traffic developing on the Snowdon Beddgelert Croesor Junction Section, although slate, metalliferous rocks, and syenite are found along the route.

Quarry and Mine ventures have not been successful in the past, but mostly owing to the difficulty of transport which the completion of the Railway would provide.

43. The completion of the system, ie the connection of the three systems, Festiniog, Croesor Branch, and North Wales Narrow Gauge, would doubtless open up a wonderful tourist route by rail through the heart of Snowdonia and would enable the proportionate cost of Rolling Stock maintenance to be lowered owing to the larger utilisation of the Workshop facilities at Boston Lodge, but since the traffic over the uncompleted portion would be seasonal passenger traffic only, it is unlikely that this traffic alone could provide a reasonable return on the cost of completion of the Railway.

The County Council at this time was concerned about the state of the roads on the overbridges at Waunfawr, Betws Garmon and Quellyn, the responsibility of the railway. In June 1921 it wrote to the NWNGR's registered office in Liverpool. Getting no reply, it did the work for £31 16s 2d (£31.81). On 15 June 1924 the NWNGR replied, 'This company is not in a position to find either the men or the materials for the repair of these roads and moreover being in chancery the Master of the Court refuses to allow any expenses except on the maintenance of the railway only. I would suggest that the County Council repair these roads themselves.'

Some NWNGR stations were renamed. Rhyd Ddu was renamed Snowdon from January 1893 and Snowdon was renamed Snowdon Ranger from July 1881 and Quellyn Lake from January 1893. In WHR days Rhyd Ddu became South Snowdon.

By the time Spring compiled his report the NWNGR had £43,040 of debentures issued, with accrued interest outstanding of just over £50,000, full debenture interest not having been paid since 1878. Neither had the company been able to repay £1,749 to holders of Lloyd's bonds and £3,487 in respect of unsecured debts, both sums due in 1888. The Dolgarrog-based Aluminium Corporation Ltd obtained control of the NWNGR in 1920. The Corporation kept the NWNGR going through 1921 by virtue of a £1,500 advance made under the auspices of Aluminium Corporation director Sir John Stewart Bt, holder of most of the debentures, to the receiver, Aluminium Corporation director Henry Joseph Jack. By this time the Welsh Highland Railway proposals were well in hand and it was obviously seen to improve the credibility of the scheme for the NWNGR to continue operating.

To purchase the undertaking in 1922, the WHR allotted £8,500 in debentures and £34,540 in ordinary shares to the NWNGR debenture holders pro rata to their holdings. Stewart received £1,500 of debentures in respect of the advance he had made to the receiver. A further £5,460 in ordinary shares was allocated to the Lloyd's bonds holders and 1888 creditors and to the debenture holders in respect of interest due. When the WHR was wound up in 1944, Stewart's estate held debentures with a face value of £9,950.

A return of £50,000 in certificates issued by a company that was, as will be seen, severely undercapitalised and which was never to make a profit, was hardly an outstanding result for some 50 years of effort. The ordinary shareholders got nothing.

Locomotives and Rolling Stock
As mentioned, the NWNGR's 1873 Act required Hugh Beaver Roberts to equip the railway with locomotives using Fairlie's Patent. Accordingly, two locomotives delivered by the Vulcan Foundry in 1875 were of this type. Built to the 0-6-4T wheel arrangement, they were designed by George Percy Spooner, designer of 0-4-4T *Taliesin* delivered to the Festiniog Railway in 1876. The

NWNGR Carriages & Wagons

names *Moel Tryfan* and *Snowdon Ranger* were applied. They had a 4½-ton axle loading and a tractive effort of 3,538lb. As built, the cabs were open to the rear but weatherboards were soon added. In 1917 the best components of the two locomotives were amalgamated to create a single locomotive called *Moel Tryfan*.

In 1878 the Hunslet Engine Co delivered another 0-6-4, this time a saddle tank, although not another Fairlie. It was named *Beddgelert* and had a tractive effort of 6,400lb. It was allegedly worn out by 1906 and was withdrawn in that year.

In 1906 the PBSSR's 2-6-2T *Russell* was delivered to the NWNGR and used by it until the establishment of the WHR in 1922.

Two years later the NWNGR replaced *Beddgelert* with another Fairlie 0-6-4T. Also obtained from Hunslet, it was later named *Gowrie* after the line's general manager and engineer. It had a tractive effort of 5,415lb. *Gowrie* was sold after World War 1, probably as surplus to requirements and, being the newest locomotive at a time when loads were light and infrequent, was seen as a quick fund-raising opportunity.

In 1917 trials took place at Dinas with a Dick Kerr petrol-electric locomotive developed to War Office requirements.

Details of the NWNGR carriage stock were not well recorded contemporarily. Two bogie brake composites and three four-wheeled passenger coaches were delivered from Ashbury Railway Carriage & Iron Co in 1874 — Charles Edwin Spooner had ordered them under Roberts's auspices. In 1877, while James Cleminson was the line's engineer, three six-wheeled composites with Cleminson Patent flexible axles were obtained from Gloucester Wagon Co. The Metropolitan

Railway Carriage & Wagon Co delivered two more bogie vehicles in 1891. They were designated as the 'workman's car' and the 'tourist carriage'. What special features distinguished the former for its purpose is not known. The second, which survives, is now better known as the 'Gladstone Car' after the politician was alleged to have ridden in it en route to opening the Watkin Path. It has two semi-open compartments either side of a central enclosed compartment that provided a matching number of seats; the idea was that passengers riding in it had a choice of seats, inside or outside, to use according to weather or inclination. The lack of ventilation in the enclosed compartment would preclude its use in the heat of summer!

Ashbury again became a NWNGR supplier in 1893, delivering two vehicles that the railway called 'corridor coaches' — this did not mean they had either corridor connections or internal corridors, merely that there was a doorway between the compartments within them. In terms of capacity the largest NWNGR rolling stock order ever placed also went to Ashbury, in 1894. The order called for four 56-seat 'summer coaches', two unglazed and two partially glazed.

The final NWNGR order for passenger rolling stock went to R. Y. Pickering & Co. That company delivered two brake composites in 1907, apparently replacing the similar 1874 vehicles; at least one of the 1874 vehicles survived as an underframe and was used on the 1941 demolition train.

For its goods traffic the NWNGR had an assortment of wagons appropriate to its traffic. Spring's paragraph No 7 gives details of the situation in 1921.

Left: A works photograph of one of the Gloucester Wagon Co's Cleminson six-wheeled third class coaches, delivered in 1878. The boards bearing the railway's name were probably affixed only for the photograph. *WHR(P)*

Right: The Gladstone Car, No 8 in the NWNGR fleet, as delivered in 1891. Officially described as a Tourist Carriage, it was built by the Metropolitan Railway Carriage & Wagon Co. *WHR(P)*

Centre right: One of the Ashbury open 'summer' coaches, delivered in 1894. *WHR(P)*

Below: Moel Tryfan and train at Rhyd Ddu. From the left are the Metropolitan 'workman's car', a Gloucester Cleminson brake/composite, an Ashbury corridor composite and a Pickering brake/composite. *Bucknall Collection*

Above: Timber bolster wagons used on the incomplete extension railway between Rhyd Ddu and Beddgelert Forest during World War 1. Photographed c1920. *Real Photographs*

Below: PBSSR under construction in 1906. The famous road bridge at Beddgelert, later abandoned by the WHR, remains a monument to past efforts to build the Porthmadog-Caernarfon railway. *P. G. Thomas/WHR(P)*

The Portmadoc, Beddgelert & South Snowdon Railway

The Portmadoc, Beddgelert & South Snowdon Railway (PBSSR) was a remarkable undertaking, having influence far beyond its achievements, and one of those was to buy a locomotive when it had no railway of its own to run it on! The PBSSR was intended to be an electric railway, the impetus for it originating with the North Wales Power & Traction Company (NWPTC). NWPTC promoted all the PBSSR Acts and Orders, claiming it was expecting to be reimbursed when the railway was completed and opened to traffic.

A full discourse on the development of the electricity supply industry is inappropriate here but the need to gain approval for building long-distance transmission lines from the NWPTC's new hydro-powered Cwm Dyli generating station was a major influence on PBSSR developments. The NWPTC wished to supply electricity to slate quarries at Blaenau Ffestiniog (Oakeley), Nantlle (Pen-yr-orsedd) and Llanberis (Dinorwic) at a time when the public was uncertain about the safety of overhead, high-tension power cables. In urban areas this fear could be overcome by building electric tramways that could eventually come into local authority ownership — offering the politicians something for very little! In the case of rural North Wales an electric railway was seen as a suitable sweetener. While the PBSSR powers did not contain reversionary provisions for the railways, they did at various times allow local authorities to buy into the schemes.

With the power station located in Nant Gwynant, near Beddgelert, it will be seen that the proposed railways radiated out in the same general directions as the NWPTC's slate quarry targets. Arguably NWPTC efforts did far more to enable the completion of the Dinas-Porthmadog link in 1923 than any previous. While the various Acts and Orders obtained might have been devised as different ways of justifying the cable routes, the idea of what became the Welsh Highland Railway had in consequence become so ingrained on the collective mind that it had to be completed, at almost any cost.

In Parliamentary terms the PBSSR story started with an Act sponsored by the North Wales & District Light Railway & Electric Power Syndicate Ltd, that received Royal Assent in 1901. The syndicate had been registered in 1900; it made applications for Light Railway Orders for a standard gauge line connecting Pwllheli with Nevin and Porthdinllaen in 1900 and 1903. In addition to incorporating the PBSSR company, the 1901 Act authorised the following:

The purchase of the Portmadoc, Croesor & Beddgelert Tram Railway Co (PCBTRC) for £10,000 within one year and the dissolution of the PCBTRC.

The continued use of the Croesor Tramway, that is the Parliamentary section, with use of 'the same or any part thereof for the conveyance and accommodation of passengers as well as of goods and mineral traffic and otherwise.'

Construction of two railways. No 1, five furlongs one chain long, was from Pen-y-mount to 'a point on the bed of the old Gorseddau Railway 87 feet or thereabouts in an easterly direction measured from the main entrance at Queen's Hotel Portmadoc'. No 2, seven miles long, commencing at a junction with the PCBTRC three miles from Portmadoc and terminating 'in a field situate at and forming part of the farm called Bwlch Mwyalchen in the parish of Beddgelert on the northerly bank of the River Glaslyn at a point adjacent to the outlet thereof to Llyn Gwynant.'

The undertaking of agreements with any or either of the Cambrian, Festiniog, NWNGR and the Snowdon Mountain Railways, for working, use and maintenance of their respective railways and other matters.

The supply of electricity to Portmadoc, Criccieth and Beddgelert and the working of the railway by electricity.

Capitalisation at £270,000 in 54,000 £5 shares, with a further £60,000 borrowing on mortgage sanctioned, supplemented by a further £30,000, in share subscriptions or loans, from four local authorities, to be repaid within 40 years.

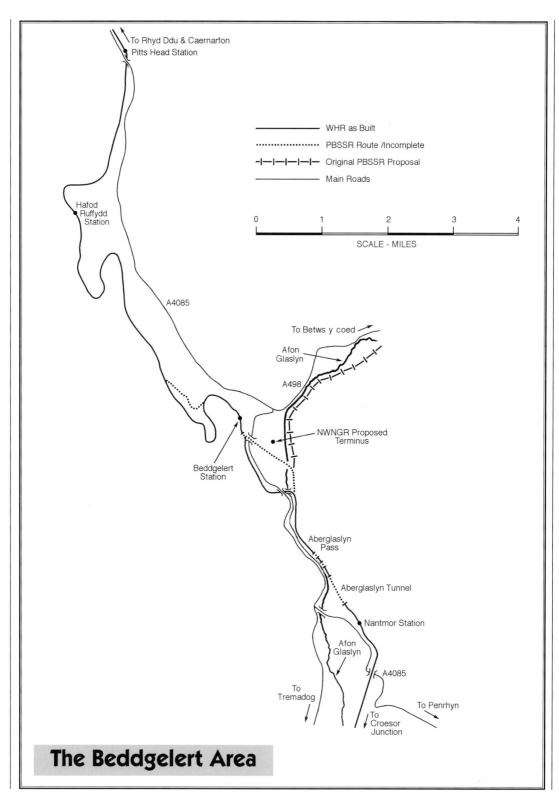

To Rhyd Ddu & Caernarfon
Pitts Head Station

WHR as Built
PBSSR Route /Incomplete
Original PBSSR Proposal
Main Roads

Hafod
Ruffydd
Station

A4085

0   1   2   3   4
SCALE - MILES

To Betws y coed

Afon
Glaslyn

A498

NWNGR Proposed
Terminus

Beddgelert
Station

Aberglaslyn
Pass

Aberglaslyn Tunnel

Nantmor Station

Afon
Glaslyn

A4085

To
Tremadog

To
Croesor
Junction

To Penrhyn

The Beddgelert Area

Right: PBSSR under construction in 1906. This is the Nantmar end of the long tunnel. The buildings on the right appear to have thatched roofs. *P. G. Thomas/WHR(P)*

Seven years were allowed for building the railways. Presumably Railway No 1 was intended to give the line a public face by the main road near to the Cambrian Railways' station. Railway No 2 would have served the power station. The Act extended the length of the Aberglaslyn tunnel from the 270yd shown on the deposited plans, to 700yd, to conceal the railway from observers standing at Pont Aberglaslyn. The company was forbidden to tip debris or rubbish on the banks of, or into, the Glaslyn between the six and seven mile points, the Aberglaslyn Pass, without the sanction of the Lord Lieutenant — an early example of environmental protection, introduced at the behest of the National Trust. Following objections, a clause of the Act gave protection for the Festiniog Railway. The PBSSR was not allowed to 'enter upon... or interfere with any portion of the railway... of' the FR and if a junction was required by the Board of Trade, at Portmadoc harbour, any additional equipment, signals etc, would be provided at PBSSR expense. (The Gorseddau Tramway was by this time abandoned; from 1856/7 it was a non-statutory 3ft gauge horse tramway, converted to 2ft gauge with Parliamentary powers obtained in 1872. Falling out of use in the 1880s, part of it survived at Porthmadog to give access to the Moel-y-gest Quarry and a stonemason's yard.)

The electricity would be generated at a hydro-electric power station located near Beddgelert, using water taken from Llyn Llydaw and Llyn Teyrn. Electricity could be supplied in bulk to any of the Cambrian, Festiniog, NWNGR, Snowdon Mountain Railways or 'any local authority, company or person authorised to supply electrical energy'. The Portmadoc and Criccieth councils could buy the installations after 36 years had elapsed from the passing of the Act.

The accounts of the electricity undertaking were to be kept separately from those of the railway. The company was allowed to acquire and hold patent and other rights in relation to the use of electrical power.

It appears that no work was carried out under this Act. The power rights were given up by the PBSSR, however, by means of the North Wales Electric Power Act of 1904, and transferred to the direct control of the NWPTC. The latter had been registered on 30 July 1903, replacing the syndicate. Bruce Peebles & Co began building the power station in 1905, generation starting the following year. The success of the electricity undertaking is shown by the fact that during the first six months of 1910 the power station sold electricity to the value of £1,833, of which £1,279 was profit!

On 22 October 1903 NWPTC minutes recorded payment of the £10,000 purchase price of the Croesor Tramway, somewhat later than the 12 months allowed by the 1901 Act for the PBSSR to complete the purchase. In 1904 a second PBSSR Act was obtained, to build further railways, to enter into agreements with the NWNGR and to obtain additional time to fulfil the railway requirements of the 1901 Act.

The new railways were conjoined to extend the NWNGR into Caernarfon. In this case the 'wrought iron or steel girder bridge' where the line passed under the LNWR was to be not less than 26ft between the parapets, one foot more than for the line authorised by the North Wales Narrow Gauge Railways (Extensions &c) Act in 1885! In September 1905 the Harbour Trustees agreed that the necessary land, that would have given the railway a frontage on the harbour and a terminal station close to the castle, could be sold for £3,000. The compulsory purchase power of the

1901 Act was extended until 1907. The approval to enter into agreements with the NWNGR was substantially a repeat of that contained in the 1901 Act. Additional capital of £24,000 was approved, with borrowing settled at one third of the issued capital after one half of the authorised capital had been issued.

Had the PBSSR fulfilled its ambitions at this stage, with its own powers and those of the NWNGR, the result would have been an electric-powered narrow gauge railway through Snowdonia, from Porthmadog to Caernarfon. As it was, there was no change at all in the position of the one completed railway owned by the PBSSR, the Croesor Tramway, and no obvious signs of action to implement the powers it had obtained for new lines.

Later in 1904 the PBSSR and the NWNGR reached agreement to transfer the latter's Beddgelert extension powers to the former, an arrangement formalised by a NWNGR extraordinary general meeting in November. It was 24 October 1906, though, before the Portmadoc, Beddgelert & South Snowdon Railway (Beddgelert Light Railway Extension) Order emerged from the Light Railway Commissioners to ratify the agreement, and for other purposes.

Meanwhile, in 1905, Ganz in Hungary started work on building 10 four-wheeled 100hp electric locomotives for the PBSSR. At least four were completed but were never delivered. Ganz later sold them for industrial use.

As stated, the 1906 Order revived the NWNGR's 1900 Beddgelert extension powers and transferred them to the PBSSR. A new railway was authorised too. It was to be six furlongs one chain (about three-quarters of a mile) long, a deviation of the 1900 line at Beddgelert, taking the line behind the Goat Hotel there and giving rise to the now famous abandoned road overbridge and abutments standing isolated in the field nearby. The function of the deviation was to ease gradients, work carried out by the NWNGR on its Beddgelert extension being formally abandoned at the same time. This route modification did not, however, eliminate three miles of 1 in 28, on reverse curves, between Beddgelert and Pitt's Head. The Aberglaslyn tunnel was again modified (the PB&SSR claiming geological difficulties prevented construction of the 1901-planned tunnel), the outcome being the three tunnels now existing. Compulsory purchase powers were valid for two years and construction was to be completed within three years. Once again, agreement could be made with the NWNGR, this time only in respect of the 1900 extension railway. However, the NWNGR power to be leased by the PBSSR, contained in the former's 1905 LRO, was repeated here too. An additional £24,000 share capital was sanctioned, together with £1,000 loan capital for each £3,000 of subscribed authorised capital. The County Council was allowed to advance not more than £2,000 by share subscription or loan. The Order was brought into effect with the seal of the Board of Trade and the signature of David Lloyd George, then its President.

Following the making of this Order, shares to the value of £50,000 were issued. A physical manifestation of progress was the order placed for the Hunslet 2-6-2T *Russell* on 13 February and delivered to the NWNGR on 29 May. Given the intention to build an electric railway and the 1905 start on electric locomotive construction, this acquisition might appear rather odd. The electric locomotives would not have been sufficiently powerful for the freight traffic, however, and the Bryngwyn service had to be

Right: Beddgelert from Bryn-y-felin, with Sygun Terrace and Nant Gwynant to the left. The freshly made PBSSR embankment, complete with contractors' track, runs alongside the Glaslyn. This route was abandoned by the WHR, which claimed that completing it, across the field behind the hedge in this photograph, would spoil the view.
W. R. Williams/ Gwyn Price Collection

GENERAL VIEW BEDDGELERT

maintained at all costs. *Beddgelert* was worn out and the Fairlies incapable, so *Russell* was the outcome. The PB&SSR clearly felt some obligation to the NWNGR, in naming the locomotive after that company's chairman and receiver, James Russell.

Under this Order, work was at last carried out, in the Aberglaslyn Pass and elsewhere around Beddgelert, Bruce Peebles having control of this. As already mentioned, some formations were completed and some track laid. Some of this work in the Beddgelert Forest, complete with track, was abandoned when the Welsh Highland Railway's 1923 deviations were built.

Two more Light Railway Orders, obtained in 1908, had the distinction of being signed by the then President of the Board of Trade, Winston S. Churchill. That made on 8 July was for an extension at Caernarfon and that made on 27 July was for an extension to Betws-y-coed. The first provided for the abandonment of part of the route at Caernarfon authorised by the 1904 Act and its substitution by a modified route along St Helen's Road, tramway style. The reason for this modification is not clear; it might have been to avoid purchase and demolition of property but it also had the added complication of crossing the LNWR's gas works and slate quay sidings on the level. The de Winton company, then in liquidation, required that the PBSSR maintain full access to their works during construction. Some land was purchased from the Harbour Commissioners in 1908, at the price agreed in 1905, for this work which was otherwise not carried out. However, that land was to be a contributory delaying factor in transferring Welsh Highland Railway assets from the Official Receiver to the Festiniog Railway Co 90 years later!

The second Order has a much more complex story and the proposed Betws-y-coed extension, called the Snowdon & Betws-y-coed Light Railway in the promotional literature, brings the NWPTC directly back into the narrative.

Firstly, the Order allowed the PBSSR railways authorised by the 1901 and 1904 Acts to be built and operated as light railways. Two newly authorised lines represented powers sought by the NWPTC in a Light Railway Order application made in November 1903. Following a public inquiry held at Corwen in July 1904, at which there was only one formal objector, the Light Railway Commissioners recommended that an Order should be made for what *The Railway Times* said would be a 28-mile railway through 'charming scenery', connecting Corwen, Betws-y-coed and Penmachno. However, when the Order was submitted to the Board of Trade for confirmation, it attracted objections from the National Trust, the Co-operative Holiday Association and the Alpine Club. A petition containing over 2,000 names of objectors was also submitted. *The Railway Times* obviously thought it significant to record that petitioners included 'members of various colleges at Oxford and Cambridge, representatives of the Universities of Wales and Manchester, and numerous residents in Manchester, Liverpool and Birmingham'. There is clearly nothing new in mass objection to railway projects. The Board later announced that the application was being held over.

By 1908 the 1903 proposal, reduced to a 12-mile route from Beddgelert to Betws-y-coed, was still also effectively a revival of part of the NWNGR's General Undertaking. The railways authorised by the 1901 and 1904 Acts were to be completed by 24 October 1909 and the Betws-y-coed line with five years of the Order. On the financial front the PBSSR's capital was reduced to £190,000 from

river crossing the formation was also complete. On the far side of Beddgelert the route to Rhyd Ddu was also substantially complete, sufficiently for it to be used (without official sanction) to haul timber out of the Beddgelert Forest later on. In 1915 it was reported that £102,668 had been expended on the PBSSR, including the purchase of the Croesor Tramway.

Later in 1909 the local authorities, tiring of the seemingly never-ending applications for powers never turning into completed railways, established an investigative committee. Two years later it was informed that the PBSSR was prepared to sell, for cash, its railway assets, land at Caernarfon, the Croesor Tramway, the incomplete railway and the extant powers. To qualify the undertaking for a Treasury grant, the LNWR provisionally agreed to construct, finish and work the line but not to finance it! The NWNGR needed to agree to LNWR involvement but Russell would not give his consent; he died at the end of 1911. By 1914 the investigative committee was known as the Portmadoc, Beddgelert & Caernarvon Light Railway Committee. In that year it decided that Caernarvon County Council should take over the Dinas to Porthmadog railway project and apply to the Light Railway Commissioners for the Portmadoc & South Snowdon Railway (Light Railway) and North Wales Narrow Gauge Railways (Light Railways) Revival and Transfer of Powers Order. The County Council, jointly with five other local authorities and the Caernarvon Harbour Trust, submitted the application in November 1914 but by then the country was at war. It was decided that further action should be deferred until peace was restored.

In 1918 the Dolgarrog-based Aluminium Corporation Ltd acquired a controlling interest in NWPTC, bringing Henry Joseph Jack into the picture and giving it control of the PBSSR. The NWPTC was renamed in May 1923, becoming the North Wales Power Co Ltd.

Thus were the foundations laid for bringing the strands together to form the Welsh Highland Railway.

£270,000, despite the additional expense of building the Betws railway. The company was not to raise more than £100,000 until a resolution to start building the Betws railway had been passed in general meeting. Subject to conditions on amounts and proportions, the company was authorised to borrow up to £130,000 on mortgage or by issuing debentures. The county council was allowed to advance a further £10,000. When the application was made, only the £50,000 of 1901 stock had been issued and none of the later issues; nothing more needs to be said about the lack of progress on the ground!

Until this point the NWPTC, the only shareholder, had financed all PBSSR activities. In terms of power transmission the 1908 orders made no sense — the only addition to the NWPTC network was made to Waunfawr in 1910 — unless it was to raise more money, improperly, for previously authorised railways. However, early in 1909 the NWPTC was unable or unprepared to continue and all work stopped. Bruce Peebles, who appears to have carried out the Beddgelert earthworks and to have started building the electric locomotives without receiving an official order, was forced into voluntary liquidation. Between Croesor Junction and the south end of the Aberglaslyn tunnels all ground works had been completed except for ballast, track and bridges. From the north end of the tunnels to the

The Welsh Highland Railway 1921—44

With the benefit of hindsight the decision to reactivate the application for the Portmadoc & South Snowdon Railway (Light Railway) and North Wales Narrow Gauge Railways (Light Railways) Revival and Transfer of Powers Order in 1921 was nothing short of bizarre. Following World War 1 much infrastructure, both transport and industry, was run-down and many companies were struggling to meet increased costs and wages. Railways were no exception, even in North Wales. That motorised road transport was on the increase, encouraged by war surplus vehicles coming onto the market cheaply, was apparently overlooked. So was the detail that the ambition of creating a narrow gauge railway link between Porthmadog and Caernarfon had been pursued for nearly 50 years with very little to show for it. Apart, that is, from a great deal of legal activity, a railway in serious decline, a horse tramway and some incomplete earthworks. However, the time was right for progress to be made even if it was not right for the achievement of success.

The Portmadoc, Beddgelert & Caernarvon Light Railway Committee met in September 1921, agreeing to reactivate the Light Railway Order application. The local authorities decided to exercise the powers available to them under the 1896 Light Railways Act to contribute loan funding to the railway, calling upon the Ministry of Transport to exercise its powers under the Act to contribute matching loan funding. The objectives, reported in the *Liverpool Daily Post* early in 1922, were to encourage the opening of small quarries along the route, open up some of the finest scenery in North Wales to tourists and for business, and, during construction, to provide 'immediate work for hundreds of the 1,800 unemployed men in the district'. The employment value of the contract eventually let was estimated to be £40,000. In September 1922 the *Daily Post* was reporting E. R. Davies as saying that 'the main purpose of the application was to effect a physical union between the two railways whereby a service should be provided without interruption running the whole way from Festiniog to Dinas,

Right: Moel Tryfan at Rhyd Ddu in 1922, with one of the first passenger trains under WHR management and one of the first since 1916. *Real Photographs*

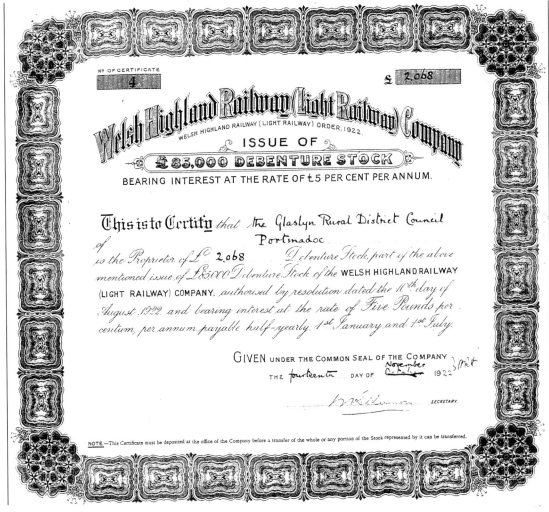

and possibly, before long, to Caernarfon.' The connection was made between the significantly larger numbers of tourists visiting the North Wales coast compared to the Cambrian coast — it was obviously expected that the railway could siphon some of these off to the benefit of all concerned.

The drive to complete the railway link was not completely of the authorities' own volition, however, but from Henry Joseph Jack. With his colleagues, Sir John Stewart Bt and Joseph Cassells from the Aluminium Company at Dolgarrog, Jack had taken control of the Festiniog Railway in June 1921. Stewart was in control, as the largest debenture holder, of the NWNGR, of which Jack was the receiver. In 1919 both Cassells and Jack were directors of the PBSSR. In 1922 Stewart became chairman of the Snowdon Mountain Railway with Jack as a director. The intention was that these railways should be electrified and run by a common (Dolgarrog-based) management. Jack was chairman of the NWPTC and a member of the County Council, later its chairman. Quoted in the *North Wales Chronicle* in January 1922, Jack said the WHR desired to put the railways in such a state that they would not continue to be a disgrace to the county.

Another name common to these boards was that of the solicitor Evan R. Davies, friend and legal colleague of David Lloyd George; Davies was also a member of the investigative committee. A further link existed in the form of Gowrie Aitchison, at various times, and sometimes simultaneously, involved with the NWNGR, the PBSSR, the NWPTC and the Snowdon Mountain Railway. He became NWNGR receiver in 1912, following Russell's death the previous year, until replaced by Jack in 1921.

On 18 October 1921 the Light Railway Commissioners held a public inquiry in Caernarfon to consider the County Council's application for an Order to authorise what was now being called the Welsh Highland Railway.

The essence of the Welsh Highland Railway (Light Railway) Order was to incorporate the Welsh Highland Railway (Light Railway) Company, and to transfer to it the undertakings and powers, reviving certain powers where appropriate, of the NWNGR and the PBSSR to create a Porthmadog-Caernarfon railway. The ambition to extend to Betws-y-coed was abandoned. An extension to Caernarfon, estimated to cost £45,000, was included but could not be undertaken without the permission of the Minister of Transport first being given in writing.

The Order was made on 1 March 1922. The company was incorporated with Stewart, Davies and Jack named as the first directors, together with two others to be nominated, one by the local authorities. The company was capitalised at £120,000 with borrowing powers being given for the same amount. The constituent railways were valued at £50,000 each, payable in shares and debentures. However, the physical assets of the NWNGR were valued at £4,000 and those of the PBSSR at £300. As already described, the NWNGR allocation was £40,000 in ordinary shares and £10,000 in debentures; £50,000 in ordinary shares were allocated in respect of the acquisition of the PBSSR. The £100,000 combined 'purchase' price of the NWNGR and the PBSSR was justified on the basis that they had a total capital value of £250,000, hence were being bought on the cheap. Festiniog Railway rolling stock was to be used to limit outlay further. In relinquishing its claims to the PBSSR and NWNGR, formally passed to Sir John Stewart, the NWPTC required wayleaves of one shilling (5p) per annum per pole or per 100yd of underground cable for any of its transmission lines built along the railway route.

WELSH HIGHLAND RAILWAY
(LIGHT RAILWAY) COMPANY.

RE-OPENING

OF

Dinas to South Snowdon

(Rhyd-ddu) Section (formerly North Wales Narrow Gauge Railway),

On 31st JULY, 1922.

10 Miles of Beautiful Scenery.

Streams, Waterfalls, Lakes & Mountains.

OBSERVATION CARS PROVIDED.

Excursion Tickets are issued daily to South Snowdon Station from Great Western Rly. Stations Via Afonwen & Dinas Jct. as follows,-

From		Times of Starting. a.m.	3rd Class Return Fare.
PORTMADOC	... ...	10 25	5s. 8d.
CRICCIETH	... ...	10 34	5s. 1d.
PWLLHELI	... ...	10 25	5s. 2d.
Arrive SOUTH SNOWDON	...	1 0 p.m.	

Passengers return as under :—

SOUTH SNOWDON STATION dept.	3 55 p.m. (Sats. exept.)	6 40 p.m.
PWLLHELI Arrive	...	6 35 p.m.	8 55 p.m.
CRICCIETH do.	...	6 32 p.m.	8 48 p.m.
PORTMADOC do.	...	6 50 p.m.	9 0 p.m.

The shortest and best ascent of SNOWDON is made from SOUTH SNOWDON STATION.
The distance is about 3 miles, and the path leads directly from the Station.

General Manager's Office, Portmadoc, Aug. 1922.

S E. TYRWHITT,
General Manager.

No. 3. Jones & Co., Printers, Portmadoc.

A Welsh Highland Heritage Copy

Continued on page 52

Left: The newly installed Bryn-y-felin bridge with the abandoned PBSSR formation parallel to the River Glaslyn behind it.
Raphael Tuck & Sons/ Gwyn Price Collection

General View of Beddgelert

Centre left: Beddgelert seen from Bryn-y-felin c1923. In the foreground the WHR track is part of the deviation authorised in the 1923 Light Railway Order to avoid spoiling the view. The route intended by the PBSSR can be calculated by extending a line from the abandoned abutments on the left. Charles Easton Spooner lies buried in the churchyard behind the church in the centre of the picture.
Gwyn Price Collection

Below: Crossing Porthmadog High Street; the end of the Baldwin-hauled train is on Junction Railway No 1 while the locomotive has crossed onto Junction Railway No 2, as defined in the Festiniog Railway's 1923 Light Railway Order.
Millbrook House Collection

ALD 305

Above: The FR's new station adjacent to the WHR in 1923, on what appears to be a busy day for passengers, probably drawn by the novelty of a new attraction. The station building is at the foot of the bank to the left, with the Snowdon Mountain Railway-run refreshment rooms behind. One of the FR's England locomotives, with a good head of steam, is on the train and standard gauge wagons on the Beddgelert Siding are discernible on the centre right. *Lilywhite/Gwyn Price Collection*

Centre right: The standard gauge crossing, showing the box maintained by the GWR with a WHR contribution, looking towards Porthmadog in 1923. *Real Photographs*

Right: At last, a train in the Aberglaslyn Pass; the Baldwin c1923. Tree growth would hinder the taking of a similar view today. *Frith/WHR(P)*

Five local authorities agreed to advance a total of £29,000, repayable by instalments over 50 years, and the Ministry of Transport an amount equal to half the total cost of completing the railway from Porthmadog to Dinas, not exceeding £37,500. For its quid pro quo the Ministry required the unskilled labour needed during construction to be obtained from the locality. The issue of interest-bearing debentures, the precise nature of which later caused some confusion within the Ministry of Transport, requiring Counsel's opinion to resolve, secured the loans. The investing authorities were authorised to borrow the money to be loaned. The value of the debentures issued eventually reached £84,774.

Tenders for construction and refurbishment were invited early in 1922, the bid of £59,985 by Sir Robert McAlpine & Sons being sanctioned. McAlpine accepted £10,000 of debentures in part payment for the fixed price contract. On 10 February 1922 the PBSSR was advertising in the *North Wales Chronicle* that it had been noticed that 'rails, sleepers and other materials' had been removed from the line. In appealing for the return of said items the notice said, 'The work of opening the Railway will be greatly simplified if this Material is returned at once'!

It will be seen that the new railway's only source of funding was the loans made by the local (investing) authorities and the Ministry of Transport. No shares were sold for cash and the loans could only be used to pay McAlpine. There was therefore no working capital, beyond any facilities provided by the bank, and no reserve. In January 1922 a spokesman for the promoters claimed they had already put £36,000 into the scheme but the source of this funding has not

been identified. It was hardly surprising that the WHR faced financial problems and hints of these were quick to emerge.

McAlpine set to work and the refurbished, to a very basic standard, NWNGR was reopened on 31 July 1922. Colonel J. W. Pringle had inspected this section on 25 July. The line had been reballasted and some sleepers and rail replaced. The original rail was identified as 41¼ lb Indian metre gauge material. Some structures had been repaired. The colonel required timber decking to be placed on both sides on the track on the 48ft underbridges — 'in view of the fact permanent way men may be working on the bridge when trains approach'

Early in 1922 the surveyors working on the 'new' route realised the gradients on the authorised PBSSR alignments around Beddgelert were not going to be suitable for steam locomotives; they had been laid out for electric traction. An application for an amendment Light Railway Order was quickly put in hand, calling primarily for two deviations, resulting in a one-day public inquiry being held in Porthmadog in September, the railway team being led by Jack.

For the railway the engineers' representative claimed that the deviations would involve less earthworks, eliminate level crossings on public roads, improve the gradient (to 1 in 40) and provide 'an altogether better route'. Jack added that 'the old route would seriously militate against the success of the railway. Any lesser cost in carrying out the original scheme would be neutralised by the increased cost of maintenance and the cost of additional works later on.' He claimed that their cost, of £7,600, was already included in McAlpine's contract.

Left: Russell at Beddgelert in 1923, still in NWNGR condition.
W. G. Rear Collection

Right: The only known extant photograph of a double Fairlie, in this case *James Spooner,* at Beddgelert.
Peter Johnson Collection

Centre right: The Baldwin, Colonel Stephens's bargain, at Dinas in 1923. *Millbrook House*

The investing authorities were concerned about the proposal in the draft Order that the new Rhyd Ddu-Croesor Junction railway should be free of rates for five years after opening. Clearly some of them expected a good revenue stream from the WHR, with rates on top of debenture interest and repayment of capital. Evan R. Davies, however, said they could not have interest in full and repayment of instalments on principal as well as rates. 'Every undertaking in its infancy has to be nursed and in its earlier years the Welsh Highland Railway will have to be carefully looked after.' That seems to be a pretty large hint that things might not work out too well. The authorities had offered to settle for two years rates-free but the railway would prefer the flexibility of not paying rates until it was in a position to pay the debenture interest and the repayment instalments. Despite two of the investing authorities threatening to withdraw their assistance, the inquiry inspector supported the railway. However, the Order as made contained no reference to this aspect of the application.

The Welsh Highland Railway (Light Railway) Amendment Order was made on 7 February 1923. The deviations were either side of Beddgelert. The first was just over two miles long and introduced two sets of reverse curves into the route between Beddgelert and Pitt's Head. The gradient became 1 in 40 instead of 1 in 28; the railway distance between the two points becoming 4 miles, compared to 2½ miles by road. Some curves had a radius as sharp as 3 chains. The other deviation was about half a mile long and took the route across the Glaslyn at Bryn-y-felin, leaving those now-famous PBSSR relics, the road overbridge and the abutments in the field, as monuments to the uncompleted railway. This deviation was made to maintain the view eastwards towards Sygyn from the road. The other item of note contained in the Order was approval for Carnarvon Corporation to loan £5,000 if the Dinas-Caernarfon railway was made. The County Council's £15,000 loan was actually conditional upon it being carried out at the earliest possible date. In November 1922 Councillor M. E. Nee, the County Council's representative on the WHR board, was telling the *North Wales Chronicle* that work on the Caernarfon extension was to start 'about April next', after the rest of the railway was finished.

The Amendment Order was not the only LRO application considered at the Porthmadog inquiry, for the Festiniog Railway required an Order too. Made on 30 January 1923, its prime function was to allow the FR to be operated as a light railway but it also authorised construction of the 'junction railways' connecting it with the WHR and a new joint station. This demonstrated a clear intention that the two railways should be worked together; Jack said it was part of the original concept of the WHR. Before the junction lines were laid, the rail journey could be made by taking a Festiniog train onto the harbour over the 1836 route and then reversing onto the Croesor Tramway. Until the opening of the Minffordd exchange sidings in 1872, slate was taken by this circuitous route for transfer to the Cambrian Railways at the Beddgelert siding. Concerned about the road crossing, Portmadoc Urban District Council submitted proposals for other routes, including that now proposed for the re-created WHR, but they were deemed impracticable; otherwise the council supported the railway. The High Street was still owned by the Tremadoc Estate, Madock's heirs, which supported the railway's proposal. Jack said that 'for the benefit of the public a bell would be provided on the engine which would ring as going through the town'. His engineering adviser, however, said that because of the low speed of the trains he did not consider it necessary to have a bell attached to the engine.

The FR Order defined two new railways, each 5 chains long. The first was across Porthmadog's widened Britannia Bridge in substitution of the existing 1836 railway located there. The bridge widening was also authorised by the Order. The

---

Welsh Highland Railway.

Suspension of Passenger Train Service.

On & from December 15th, 1924, and until further notice, the passenger train service on the Welsh Highland Railway, shewn in the Company's Time Tables, dated September 1924, will be discontinued.

Goods and parcels traffic will continue to be dealt with, except that Perishable Traffic will **NOT** in future be accepted for conveyance.

For particulars of goods train service, and times of acceptance and delivery of goods and parcels, see notices exhibited at the Stations.

Portmadoc,
1st Dec., 1924.

E. H. R. NICHOLLS,
Manager.

No 89.   Lloyd & Son, Printers, Portmadoc.

---

second railway linked the first 'across High Street and along Madoc Street' to the WHR. McAlpine undertook this work also, accepting FR debentures in part payment. The new station, estimated to cost £3,000, was intended to be a substitute for Harbour station and the Boston Lodge Works facility was intended to be relocated there too. Although often described as the WHR station, it was in fact, despite being located on the WHR, a Festiniog Railway station, known at first as Porthmadog (New). In 1923 FR trains terminated there, instead of at Harbour station.

The complete railway was opened on 1 June 1923, three months later than intended. McAlpine had been unable to employ sufficient experienced local labour to meet the railway's obligations in that respect. More rock had required removing than calculated and access to some land had been protracted. At least one land dispute carried on for several years. McAlpine was contracted to buy any necessary land and convey it to the railway. The owners of Beddgelert's Royal Goat Hotel, Tourists Hotels Ltd, and others perhaps, claimed not to have been paid for their land near Beddgelert station. When they approached the

Left: Admission of defeat? Certainly so far as the passenger service was concerned. *Welsh Highland Heritage*

Above: Cilgwyn, a source of traffic for the WHR, seen in the 1930s. *WHR(P)*

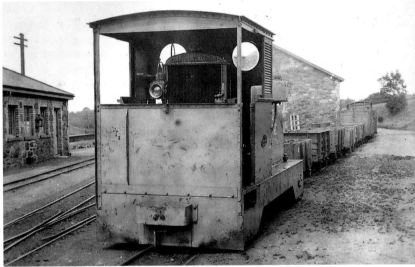

Right: Kerr Stewart's prototype diesel locomotive on test at Dinas in 1928, when it spent some time operating Bryngwyn branch traffic, as seen here. *LGRP*

railway for payment they were told the complaint was with McAlpine. The capital cost of construction, including legal, parliamentary and other fees, interest, land purchases and the works, was £70,332.

The WHR intended to reopen the Bryngwyn branch to passengers but this was never done. The revived railway was launched with Jack as Chairman, Davies and Stewart as directors and M. E. Nee, a Caernarfon solicitor and county councillor, as director representing the investing authorities. Except for Mr Nee, the same persons directed the Festiniog and the Snowdon Mountain Railways.

Lt-Col A. H. L. Mount inspected the remainder of the line on 24 May 1923, the company having

run a 'successful trial trip' with a Fairlie and three coaches on 15 May, as reported in a local newspaper. The guest list on that occasion included Jack, Evan R. Davies, S. E. Tyrwhitt, General Manager, Alfred McAlpine, the contractor, and J. K. Prendergast, of the engineers Sir Douglas Fox and Partners.

Mount submitted an 11-page report on the 12½ miles of railway that he inspected. He listed all sidings and loops, measuring from Rhyd Ddu. Slightly more than half a mile of the route from Rhyd Ddu had refurbished pre-existing track. The Croesor Tramway section was described as being in good order, only requiring replacement of 500 sleepers; the rail was 41lb flat-bottom. Damage to the existing sleepers by horses' hooves was forecast

to limit their potential lives. On the 'new' line new 40lb flat-bottom rail had been used, although on some of the sharper curves it had not been properly bent and was tending to spring out of alignment.

He tested the Bryn-y-felin bridge under load with two (Festiniog) Fairlies, weighing 21 and 24 tons at 15mph — regrettably any photographs that might have been taken appear not to have survived. He recommended that the bridges be painted but they never were.

At the level crossing over the GWR at Porthmadog, Mount discussed working arrangements with a GWR representative. On the standard gauge there were about 40 movements per day; on the narrow, during construction, about 20. Trap points on the WHR protected the GWR. A woman employed by the GWR had operated the crossing but with the coming of

narrow gauge passenger trains it had become a posting for a porter signalman, with telephone communication to Porthmadog East signalbox.

Noting that there was still a considerable amount of work to be done, Mount recommended approval for passenger trains for a temporary period of six months. At the end of that period the complete line, and the FR, should be reinspected.

The junction railways and the new station were also inspected on 24 May. The direct Croesor Tramway line to the harbour had been retained, on a new alignment, and with the FR harbour line and the junction railways formed a triangular layout in the road at the High Street/Madoc Street junction. Neither the inspector nor the council approved of the points and flangeways provided. Lt-Col Mount mistakenly described the new line over the Britannia Bridge as being a realignment of the Croesor Tramway. The track here and in Madoc

Street was proud of the road surface and was causing the local authority concern about drainage. Mount agreed that a kerb would help drainage, with the added benefit of separating the railway from road users, and commended it to the railway. He recommended temporary approval for passenger trains but it was to be several years before the council was satisfied with the condition of the road.

On 1 April 1923, just before the line opened, Col Stephens was appointed civil engineer and locomotive superintendent of both the Festiniog and Welsh Highland Railways. He quickly made his mark by arranging for the acquisition of an ex-War Department Baldwin 4-6-0T, that arrived at Dinas on 4 July 1923. The FR's ex-WD 45hp Simplex tractor, now named *Mary Ann*, was also tried out on the WHR in 1923. The *Railway Gazette* reported trials taking place during which they saw the loco running the length of the WHR, including the Bryngwyn branch.

The new railway was launched with advertisements in local newspapers and the distribution of handbills. In the current jargon, 'marketing' was handled by the Snowdon Mountain Railway, which produced a pictorial poster notable for a lack of railway content in its design, picture postcards and the 128-page *Snowdon and Welsh Highland Holiday Book*. Produced before the railway was opened, the latter contained details of the FR as well as the railways of its title. Aspects of the WHR route were illustrated by paintings made by an artist unfamiliar with the appearance of steam locomotives and trains. The *Official Souvenir to the Snowdon & Welsh Highland Railways*,

published circa 1925, was concerned mainly with the SMR and contained only brief details of the WHR and the FR. The SMR ran the refreshment facilities at Porthmadog (New) and Dinas stations.

Once trains started running, the accounts soon failed to add up in a positive direction. A revenue loss in 1922, with only the NWNGR section open, was more than doubled in 1923, when the whole line was operated, and this despite a tenfold increase in passenger revenue. The Joint Committee of the Investing Authorities unmistakably disliked the results and in 1925 produced a list of 19 strongly worded questions to which it required answers. Loco mileage was 55,546 in 1924, consuming 862 tons of coal, 64 miles per ton, compared with 16,850 miles for 189 tons, 89 miles per ton, in 1922. Whether the 1 in 40 gradients were the only reason for this change in fuel economy is open to speculation. Including the Dinas stationmaster, paid 85s (£4.25) per week, train operating was in the hands of seven men. The railway employed seven others on weekly pay and one loader paid on a tonnage basis. Stephens was paid £100 a year, as was the company secretary. A percentage of the FR's overheads was paid, including a proportion of salaries of the managing director (E. R. Nicholls), assistant to managing director (R. Evans), shorthand typist, storekeeper, clerk, loco superintendent, permanent way inspector and Porthmadog stationmaster. None of the directors had received any fees.

The final question asked by the investing authorities was 'if information could be given of the present financial position of the Company'.

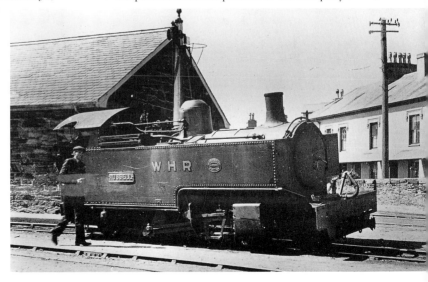

Right: Russell at Harbour station in 1936. The FR applied this paint scheme after the start of the 1934 lease.
S. W. Baker/WHR(P)

The response was, 'The success of the Railway depends upon the development of the mineral traffic. A new Granite Quarry has been opened at Betws Garmon and a new Copper Mine is about to be opened at Nantmor. The expenses of running are kept down to the bare minimum and if the local authorities with their local knowledge and influence could help in getting two or three Mines and Quarries started the Company should be able to pay its debenture interest.'

Jack was blamed for the lack of success and accepted responsibility, with his resignation effective from 1 November 1924. Stephens became a director on 20 November and on 1 January 1925 added the roles of chairman and managing director to his portfolio.

WHR passenger traffic actually peaked in 1923, with 58,203 tickets being issued. The only payment of debenture interest, £4,238, was made the same year. Following a reduction in the tickets issued to 50,485 in 1924, it was decided to cease winter passenger working with immediate effect. Thereafter a restricted winter service operated each year until 1930, when ticket sales had declined to 1,599.

The only rolling stock the WHR brought to the combined system was the former NWNGR equipment. It was higher than the Festiniog stock and the two railways had incompatible brakes and couplings. In the beginning attempts were made to work trains throughout the system and at first FR stock did work through to Dinas. In the other direction the NWNGR carriages were reduced in height to allow them to work through the FR's tunnels. On the locomotive front, however, the FR became notorious for the failed and unsympathetic attempt made to extend *Russell's* operating range by reducing it to the FR loading gauge. It was not long, therefore, before the 'new' line was divided between the two systems, Beddgelert being the boundary. Writing in their 1941 WHR valediction published in the *Railway Magazine*, C. Hamilton Ellis and Charles E. Lee said Beddgelert was treated as a sort of frontier station.

The state of the road surfaces on the NWNGR overbridges came to attention on 29 May 1924, when the County Council estimated they could be repaired for £845 8s 0d (£845.40) and maintained for £88 per annum. The railway replied on 8 September 1924, saying that the financial position precluded the railway taking action and suggesting the council dealt with the situation. The work was carried out by 21 June 1927, after the railway had agreed to take out a bond as security for the council's expenses. Col Stephens was later to write a strongly worded letter to the council, complaining about the state of the road surfaces on the bridges! The Bryn-y-felin road bridge was omitted from the council's responsibilities and became the subject of a police complaint in July 1933.

Continued on page 68

Views Along the Line Porthmadog to Dinas

Right: The Baldwin pulls on to the FR from the WHR, probably in the 1930s. The loco was too large to go beyond Boston Lodge. *Peter Johnson Collection*

Centre right: Welsh Pony stands by the goods shed at the FR's Harbour station, waiting to leave for the WHR, in 1934. *Real Photographs*

Left: On 8 August 1935 the Baldwin pulls its train into Madoc Street, heading for the WHR. *H. F. Wheeller/ Adrian Gray Collection*

Lower right: A Festiniog Fairlie running round its train at Portmadoc New (1923) in 1932. *W. G. Rear Collection*

Left: The Baldwin at Portmadoc New (1929) c1936. Standard gauge wagons on the Beddgelert Siding are visible on the right.
C. R. L. Coles/Millbrook House

Centre left: Passengers disembarking from a *Russell*-hauled train at Portmadoc New (1929) in 1934.
Real Photographs

Below: Croesor Junction in 1925. The WHR turned to the left and the Croesor Tramway, with wagons just discernible alongside a NWPT pylon, ran straight on. *C. L. Mowat/ Adrian Gray Collection*

Above right: Nantmor station and *Russell* with a short passenger train heading for Porthmadog in 1923; *Russell* is still in NWNGR condition, station painting is incomplete and fencing unfinished.
Commercial postcard/ W. G. Rear Collection

Below right: A train disappears into the Aberglaslyn Pass from Nantmor in 1935.
H. F. Wheeller/ Millbrook House

Left: Russell and a well-laden train in the Aberglaslyn Pass. The picture demonstrates the magnitude of the tunnel bore in relation to the size of the trains. *Ifor Higgon/ Millbrook House*

Centre left: The Bryn-y-felin bridge, fitted with the walkways required by Lt-Col Mount but still unpainted. *Peter Johnson Collection*

Below left: Emitting both steam and smoke, an England loco attracts the attention of a family group at Bryn-y-felin. *Peter Treloar Collection*

Above right: Beddgelert in 1936. *Russell's* rear cabsheet has been the beneficiary of some remedial platework. The NWNGR summer car is empty and the buffet car still has room for plenty more passengers. *Real Photographs*

Below right: Russell and *Welsh Pony* at Beddgelert in 1934. *R. W. Kidner/ W. G. Rear Collection*

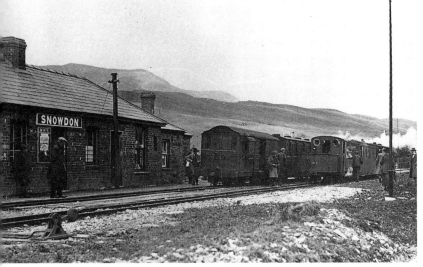

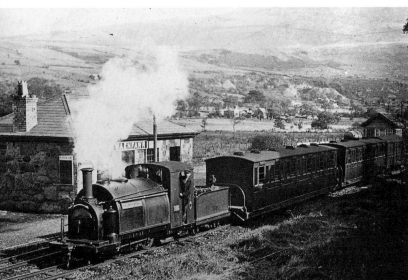

Left: Festiniog stock, locomotive and carriages, at Rhyd Ddu in 1923.
Peter Johnson Collection

Centre left: Palmerston and a train of Festiniog carriages at Waunfawr in 1923.
Topical Press/FR Archives

Below left: A mixed train at Waunfawr, with a Festiniog bowsider coupled next to *Moel Tryfan*.
Ken Nunn Collection

Right: In 1934 a horse, right, was startled by the sound of *Russell* and train approaching Waunfawr from Dinas.
W. G. Rear Collection

Below right: Tryfan Junction is the location of this picture of *Palmerston* and its FR train in 1923. *Topical Press/ W. G. Rear Collection*

Having approved the WHR for passenger traffic for a temporary six-month period in 1923, Lt-Col Mount returned and reinspected the line on 6 September 1926, three years later. Subject to some minor works, he recommended that both the WHR between Rhyd Ddu and Porthmadog and the Festiniog's junction railways be approved for passenger traffic. He also approved the works on the Britannia Bridge, despite their not being as he recommended, and noted that the direct, Croesor, line to the harbour had been removed, eliminating the triangular layout.

Operating the crossing over the GWR proved not to be as straightforward as might have been expected. As already mentioned, the GWR had upgraded its status with the advent of the WHR and commenced billing the railway for its use, where previously there had been no charge. In 1928 the matter went to court, the GWR claiming that the standard gauge was on the site before the narrow. (Croesor Tramway opened in 1864; Cambrian Railways opened in 1867.) The claim was based on the deposited plans for the standard gauge not showing the tramway although the plan on the conveyance, effected in 1879, did show it. The GWR further claimed that the Croesor crossing was a product of its Borth-y-Gest extension, sanctioned by its 1885 Act. The

Cambrian and then the GWR had always paid for the crossing keeper and had never sought payment but the coming of the WHR put a more onerous responsibility on the GWR and the company wanted compensating for it. The WHR was unable to establish its case and had to pay for the service. To save money, passenger trains ceased to use the crossing from 1929, when a basic platform was established alongside the Beddgelert Siding.

In 1927 Tourists Hotels Ltd, in liquidation, succeeded in an action brought against the railway for breach of contract in respect of a covenant made to provide an access road across the railway to land that the Hotels company wished to sell as housing plots, Tourist Hotels being awarded £1,000. To protect their interests the investing authorities met on 12 February that year. They resolved 'that the Clerk of the County Council be authorised to take the necessary steps, for the appointment of a Receiver and Manager, or by proceedings, to protect the interests of the Investing Authorities; all the Investing Authorities to pay their share of the expenses incurred, and that the name of Col Stephens, the Managing Director of the Company, be submitted for consideration'. The claim of Tourists Hotels Ltd, then £1,150, was

Left: The main line to Porthmadog runs through the centre of this view of Dinas loco shed and signalbox. The carriage sheds are on the left and the standard gauge line to Afon Wen on the right. *Peter Johnson Collection*

Right: Interchange at Dinas — passengers, on 4 August 1936. *W. H. Whitworth/ Peter Johnson Collection*

Above: Interchange at Dinas — slate, early 1920s. *Topical Press/ Real Photographs*

Right: In 1934 railway employees pose for photography with *Russell* while a passenger peers at the locomotive's footplate. *Real Photographs*

still outstanding at the winding-up in 1944. After the 1924 payment no interest was ever paid to the investing authorities, nor was any part of the loans repaid to them.

The investing authorities decided on 16 December 1930 to approach the LMS and the GWR to see if either company would take over and operate the WHR. Neither would. A net loss of £218 was made during the year. Nothing done for the railway had worked out — a nominal £1,200 deposited against the Caernarfon extension and invested in government stocks was worth only £700 in 1931 when Stephens was in correspondence with the County Council about getting it released to the revenue account.

Col Stephens died on 23 October 1931, the settlement of his affairs with the railway being protracted and dragging on until 1944; in 1933 it was established that his estate was due £691, including arrears of salary. J. A. Iggulden, of Stephens's Tonbridge office, took over as receiver and manager for six months, until Caernarfon accountant R. T. Griffith was appointed receiver. He was also clerk to Gwyrfai Rural District Council, one of the investing authorities. On 23 March 1932 Iggulden wrote to the County Council that there were insufficient funds for the railway to renew its third party insurance policy at £35. By return the council offered to advance the £35 but by then Iggulden had a coal bill, £12 and the locomotive boiler insurance renewal premium, £6, to pay. Stephens's assistant,

W. H. Austen, was Stephens's successor as engineer and locomotive superintendent.

At the end of the 1933 summer season no future could be seen for the railway. With an input from the investing authorities, its closure was announced to take effect from 1 January 1934.

Continuous attempts were made, including approaches to the Ministry of Transport, to encourage the quarries to send their output via the WHR. On 19 January 1934 the County Council held a meeting with the manager, O. W. Owen, of the Caernarvonshire Crown Slate Quarries Company, operators of Cilgwyn, Braich, Moel Tryfan and Alexandra quarries since 2 August 1932. Cilgwyn output could reach Bryngwyn Drumhead via a tramway, arriving at Dinas Junction after two days and incurring a cost of 11s (55p) per ton. The company had built a road from the quarry, linking it to the road serving Pen-y-groes station on the former Carnarvonshire Railway; using it, the journey time to Pen-y-groes was 20min by motor lorry and the cost 2s 9d (14p) per ton. Moel Tryfan quarry, however, had a direct connection to the Drumhead and its transport thence cost only 2s 8d (13p) per ton. Despite the WHR's 4s (20p) per ton for the Drumhead-Dinas journey, the railway was a cost-effective means of shipment from Moel Tryfan. The company expected to link the Alexandra quarry, not then in production, to Moel Tryfan by road and then send its output by WHR also.

Above left: Beddgelert station still looking cared for. The building at right angles to the track was the bookstall. The lorry belonged to the village coal merchant. *F. Frith/WHR(P)*

Above: Everything stops for the photographer, c1930. The 'station mistress' in Welsh national costume, standing next to *Little Giant,* was the WHR equivalent of Tan-y-bwlch's Bessie Jones. Wagons loaded with coal await attention from the coal merchant. By now the bookstall had been removed. *Commercial postcard/ Peter Johnson Collection*

Unfortunately, the slate industry was set for another of its periodic depressions.

Responding to a good 1934 season on its own line the FR decided to run the WHR directly, with a 42-year lease made on 26 June 1934, taking over from 1 July. The FR was to pay £1 for the first half year and then 10% of the gross income as rent for the following 13 years. For the next 7½ years the rent was to be 10% of the gross income plus 5% of any gross income exceeding £2,000. Thereafter the rent was to be reviewed. Had WHR traffic picked up as expected, this would have been a reasonable deal, although it was still unlikely to earn enough to pay debenture interest. For the FR it was a disaster, committing it to pay rent even if the WHR made no operating profit. The lease detailed all the WHR's assets, including two broken clocks at Beddgelert! It excluded the land acquired by the PBSSR at Caernarfon. Evan R. Davies arranged the lease for the FR; regrettably he died before the year's end.

Despite the lease and reopening, 1934 was not a good one for the WHR company. Stephens's executors issued a summons for the moneys due to the estate; by October the bank account was overdrawn and the bank told the receiver, Griffith, that it held him personally responsible for the shortfall. Not unnaturally he thought this was unfair and offered to settle by instalments. On the railway the FR painted the carriages in different bright colours and offered a special through fare from Dinas to Blaenau Ffestiniog, on different trains either side the of GWR at Porthmadog. It failed to compete, however, with road competition offering a more spectacular route over the Llanberis Pass and similar roads.

On 31 December 1936, W. Cradoc Davies, then FR company chairman, met with the investing authorities. The FR had run the WHR for 2½ years and wanted to be freed from the lease. He said the track was in poor condition when the FR took it over and needed a 'substantial sum of money' spending on it; 1934 produced a loss of £506. In 1935 Moel Tryfan Quarry stopped using the railway. One train a week sufficed for coal and groceries traffic, covering its cost. 1935 receipts were £1,001, producing a loss of £596 including the 10% rent. At 30 September 1936, when the seasonal passenger service ended, revenue had been £1,033, against costs of

Continued on page 74

Above: Little Giant on a train of Festiniog stock in 1923. *Bucknall Collection*

Below: Russell and the Baldwin in 1935. The Gladstone Car is coupled next to *Russell*. *Peter Johnson Collection*

Right: Close-up of the station building in the 1930s. Note the bottles of pop on display in the window.
J. T. Suffield/via David Waldren

Centre right: This strange scene, dating from July 1936, has *Russell* and the Baldwin facing each other on the same track! Presumably this is part of the run-round procedure when trains from north and south both terminated at Beddgelert. Alongside the Baldwin the local coal merchant can be seen loading his lorry.
H. B. Tours/Festiniog Railway Heritage Group Collection

Below right: Russell with a midday arrival on a hot 8 August 1935. It was patently expected to be a busy day, for there are five carriages in the train. *Russell* is also missing its sand bucket. *H. F. Wheeller/ Millbrook House*

£1,283. A weekly goods train run after that period had to be taken into account, a proportion of overheads and the 10% rent added too. The WHR faced strong bus competition and took twice as long to make the journey.

The FR made a loss of £105 in 1935, after allowing for the WHR's 10%; without it both lines would have cleared their expenses. From March 1936 the Blaenau Ffestiniog quarrymen were on strike for nine weeks, during which the FR continued operating to clear stocks from the quarries; at the end of the year the FR was £1,000 worse off than it had been the previous year. Most FR passengers were from the North Wales coast, travelling via the Conwy Valley; a fair percentage travelled through to Dinas. Very few joined the WHR from the LMS at Dinas. The LMS had an interest in Crosville and encouraged its passengers to take the bus at Blaenau Ffestiniog — the FR objected to this and traffic picked up. The WHR lost FR passengers to the buses at Porthmadog, despite the railway's best efforts. The situation became worse in 1937 because Crosville had erected additional stands alongside the platform at Blaenau Ffestiniog. The investing authorities asked Davies to submit the FR's case for being freed from the lease in writing. The authorities would pass this on to the Treasury and the Ministry of Transport; if they were agreeable, the authorities would make an application for approval for the receiver not to press for the rent

but the authorities would not, at this stage, agree to the lease being relinquished.

Davies's letter was discussed at a further meeting of the investing authorities held at Caernarfon on 29 April 1937. It had been forwarded to the Ministry of Transport and a meeting had taken place with an officer of the Ministry's Finance & Statistics Department. It was suggested that the WHR company be wound up, subject to court approval, and the assets realised; the FR should pay a lump sum in addition to the rent due at the time of release. At Caernarfon this course of action was agreed, the sum payable by the FR being set at £500.

The individual investing authorities were required to pass resolutions agreeing to the WHR being wound up. Deudraeth Rural District Council's clerk wrote that 'the Council have all along been in favour of doing away with this railway'. Portmadoc UDC asked for first option of purchasing the rails between Porthmadog and Croesor Junction, as without the railway, 'it would be practically hopeless to expect the Park, Croesor and Rhosydd Slate Quarries to be reopened ... no approach roads were ever constructed ... whereby road transport could ... bring their produce to market'.

The County Council, acting for the investing authorities and the debenture holders, formally put the proposal that the FR should be freed from the lease in exchange for a payment of £500 and outstanding rent to the company on 22 November 1937. Taking some time to establish its position, the FR responded on 15 February 1938. The letter was signed by Company Secretary Cynan Evan Davies, a son of Evan R. Davies, Secretary from 1924 until 1955, a signatory of the 1934 lease and managing director of the Snowdon Mountain Railway since 1930. He reviewed the situation and said that the rent now due was about £210, which the FR was unable to pay or to borrow. He made a counter-offer of £600 in full discharge of all claims, payable in three annual instalments, recognising that there was no way of telling if the company would be able to fulfil the obligation being offered.

He went on to ask if the FR could keep *Moel Tryfan*, then lying dismantled at Boston Lodge. Davies said it had never worked during the period of the lease, having failed its insurance examination in July 1934, and could only be reconditioned at considerable expense; he further claimed that some work had been done on reconditioning parts of the locomotive at Boston Lodge. In closing, Davies laid claim to the railway between 'our Portmadoc station and the GWR main line'. This length was put down at the expense of the FR, he said, claiming the right to remove rails and sleepers along it. The claim, eventually accepted, was wrongly made, as the boundary between the FR's 1923 junction railway and the WHR was where the route left Madoc Street. By this time the GWR line had become the most practical boundary, due to that company having, apparently without consultation, removed the crossing!

Iggulden's correspondence with the council, meanwhile, with respect to both Stephens's estate and his own salary, £50, due to him for his six-month tenure as receiver and manager, was as drawn out as anything else to do with the WHR. On 9 March 1939 he threatened to remove rail to the value of the sum outstanding on Stephens's estate. The County Council replied on 6 June saying that 'several enquiries have been received in respect of same' (the rail, most of the South Snowdon-Croesor Junction section was laid with rail less than 20 years old and it had seen very little use) and that the authority's London agent was to obtain the instruction of the court concerning the sale of track materials. George Cohen, Sons & Co had offered £3,815 on 3 May

for 'track, rolling stock, sleepers, buildings, telegraph poles and wire, etc.' Iggulden's salary claim still had not been settled two years later.

There matters rested until the war and continued requests to the County Council concerning the rail prompted further action. Counsel's opinion was sought on 23 May 1940, seeking legal clarification on six points. W. Gordon Brown QC delivered his opinion on 5 June. It would not be possible to get a Board of Trade winding-up order under Section 7 of the Light Railways Act 1912, because inability to carry on the undertaking arose from financial difficulties, not from the sale of the undertaking. The undertaking, anyway, could not be sold without the authority of Parliament. The railway company could be wound up under Section 338 of the Companies Act 1929; provided the FR's lease was determined first, the liquidator could then discontinue working the railway and realise the assets. An abandonment order would not be necessary before presenting a winding-up petition. He was unable to determine who should best petition for a winding-up order. Finally he opined that the receiver could not be held personally responsible for any loss sustained by landowners or tenants in respect of abandoned cuttings, nor could he be compelled to repair fencing.

The final points arose because one of the abandoned PBSSR cuttings had become waterlogged, the farmer holding the railway liable when his sheep fell in and drowned.

In January 1941 the County Council's London solicitor wrote reporting on a meeting held with the Chief Clerk at Chancery Chambers. Officials had pointed out that the company should not have abandoned the undertaking without statutory powers. 'On the other hand it was pointed out that if in fact the Ministry of Supply should formally requisition under the Emergency Powers the rails then the Receiver can afterwards come to the Court for the necessary directions on the footing that he is no longer able to carry on the undertaking, the rails having been acquired by the Ministry.' This opinion cleared the way for the track disposal, formalised by a Ministry of Supply requisition order dated 13 March 1941. The order covered the railway and sidings (except for the Croesor section), all equipment at Dinas, goods wagons, 50 wheel sets, two steam locomotives and various scrap items lying around the permanent way. A supplementary order issued on 1 August 1941 referred to the coaches and other rolling stock. The requisitioned assets were sold to George Cohen, Sons & Co; this company

Continued on page 80

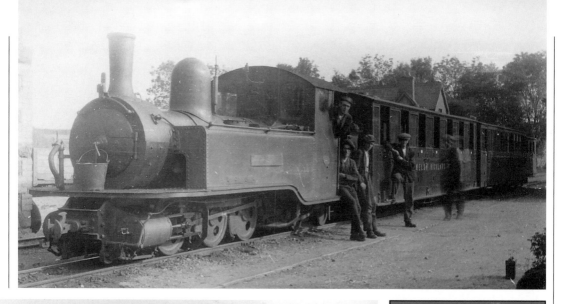

Locomotives

Above: Moel Tryfan and train at Dinas on 11 June 1925. The Fairlie's cab roof has been modified to fit the FR's loading gauge and the lower smokebox has been patched.
A. W. Croughton/ Millbrook House

Left: Russell, still in NWNGR condition, seen at Beddgelert in 1923.
Peter Johnson Collection

Below left: Russell in post-lease condition at Dinas c1935. Obviously a warm day, as the loco crew have removed the cab backsheet The 1920s modifications to the 'top line', in the failed hope of getting it to fit through the FR tunnels, are obvious.
Millbrook House

Right: Another 1935 view of *Russell*. The number 12 was applied to *Russell* by the FR in 1934. *R. Priestley/WHR(P)*

Centre right: Russell in exile, on Fayle's Tramway, Dorset, in 1950. New nameplates had been made for it because the originals had been given to the LNER Railway Museum at York. *WHR(P)*

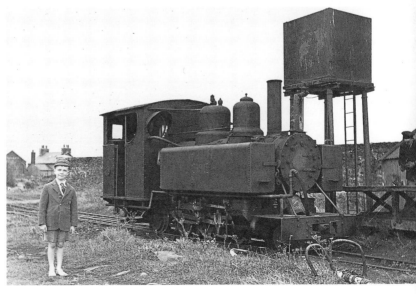

Below right: The Baldwin in 1936, at the FR's Harbour station water tower.
E. R. Morten

Left: In July 1936 the Baldwin was seen during a stop at Portmadoc New (1929); the driver takes the opportunity to oil round. To the right is Gelert's Farm, the site now owned, with the Beddgelert Siding, by Welsh Highland Railway Ltd (WHR(P)).
H. B. Tours/
Adrian Gray Collection

Centre left: Consideration was given to reacquiring *Gowrie* in 1923 and an inspection was carried out. It was photographed at Wake's Yard in Darlington on 11 October 1926. *Real Photographs*

Below: The Baldwin and *Moel Tryfan* at Dinas in the 1920s, showing the differences in height allowed by the NWNGR/WHR and FR loading gauges. Most likely post-1923 loco turning was undertaken using the Boston Lodge turntable.
Goronwy Roberts/WHR(P)

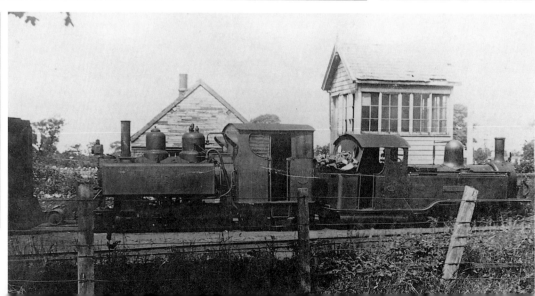

Right: All the FR's England engines active after 1923 saw service on the WHR, this view of *Welsh Pony* at Beddgelert in the 1930s representing them in this section. The building on the left was used as a store; that on the right was the goods shed. *Millbrook House*

Above: A further contrast in size is presented by the pairing of the Baldwin with *Little Giant* alongside Dinas carriage shed in 1923.
Real Photographs/WHR(P)

Right: Bought in 1925, the Baldwin tractor was Army surplus. It is seen outside the flour mill in Porthmadog in the 1930s. Returned to light service on the FR in 1998, the locomotive is named *Moelwyn* on that railway.
Real Photographs

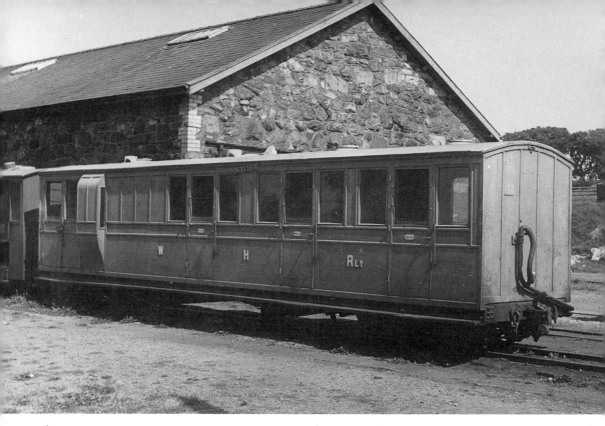

started on site in August 1941 and worked through until the following year. Track at Hafod Ruffydd, between Pitt's Head and Beddgelert, was left in situ and made available for the War Department to use for mobile target practice by shooting at slate wagons.

In September 1941 the County Council's solicitor and clerk was preparing the summons freeing the FR from its lease for presentation to the High Court. £200 of the £600 was to become due immediately the lease was surrendered, the remainder one year after the end of the war or from the date of any armistice, whichever happened first, payable in four annual instalments. The order gave the FR all rights pertaining to the junction railways.

A legal hiatus occurred in 1942 when on 16 April further opinion was received from W. Gordon Brown QC. Generally speaking, he thought the wrong approaches were being used to secure both the freeing of the FR from the lease and a winding-up order for the WHR. An added complication arose because the WHR had no surviving directors. Walter Cradoc Davies, Ralph Freeman (the civil engineer) and Crossley Colley (of Conwy) were appointed by the court. However, at a hearing on 3 November that year the FR gained approval to agree to surrender the

lease — it appeared that there were no powers to force the FR to surrender it. The surrender was formalised by an agreement with the receiver dated 12 August 1943, whereby the FR agreed to pay £550, still by instalments, instead of the original £600!

On 26 January 1944 the County Council petitioned the High Court for a winding-up order in respect of the WHR. The hearing took place on 7 February, when Mr Justice Uthwatt made the order. The County Council's London solicitor reported that there was some considerable argument as to whether the court had power to make the order. The petition stated that the only assets were £12,800 received for the requisitioned stock and equipment and the £550 due from the FR. (In the *Liverpool Daily Post* for 8 February 1944, and elsewhere, the figure for the requisitioned stock was given as £1,280 — the figure of £12,800 is given in two official documents seen by the author.)

The total deficiency of the WHR at 4 March 1927, when a receiver was appointed, was given as £175,171, of which £150,877 was in respect of land, buildings, permanent way and (unspecified) equipment, written down to £20,000 in 1944. Amongst the unsecured creditors were the FR, owed £1,036, and the NWNGR, owed £1,081.

Carriages & Wagons

Left: No 8, One of the 1907-built Pickering brake composites, at Dinas on 8 August 1935. A 'Dinas' destination board is mounted in a fixing on the cant rail.
H. F. Wheeller/
Adrian Gray Collection

Above: A train at Nantmor, consisting of a Pickering brake composite and an 1894 summer car. Note the different style of lettering on the Pickering vehicle to that on No 8, seen on the same day. The permanent way trolley is attached to the train by rope!
H. F. Wheeller/Millbrook House

Centre right: The Gladstone Car, a semi-open summer car and a Pickering brake composite in the 1930s, all painted different colours.
Peter Johnson Collection

Right: 1894-built Ashbury corridor coach at Dinas on 8 August 1935. *H. F. Wheeller/*
Adrian Gray Collection

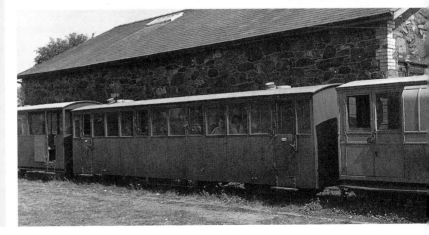

The Kent & East Sussex Railway and the North Devon & Cornwall Railway, parts of the Col Stephens empire, were owed money, as was the Snowdon Mountain Railway. Caernarvonshire County Council was owed £630 due for repairing the roads over the NWNGR bridges. The Shropshire & Montgomeryshire Railway, another part of Stephens's empire, owed the WHR £4.

Of the £90,000 ordinary share capital issued to secure the NWNGR and PBSSR undertakings, £26,696 was held by the estate of Evan R. Davies and £52,891 by the estate of Henry Joseph Jack. The next largest holdings, each of £1,430, were registered to William D. Penrot and others of Finchley and the executors of C. V. T. Hodgson.

Debts

Unsecured creditors	£6,521
Preferential creditors	£1,494
Debentures	£84,774
Interest to 4/3/27	£13,300
Shares	£90,000
Total	£196,089

Left: Carriage cleaning at Dinas. The circumstances surrounding this photograph, one of a series, are unknown. Presumably there is some prewar railway volunteering going on. *WHR(P)*

Below: Assorted wagons and vans make up a goods train at Dinas in 1923. At the right is an FR coal wagon. *Real Photographs*

Assets

Cash	£125
Stock	£25
Land, buildings, p/way, equipment at cost	£170,877
Stamp duties	£2,316
Debts	£768
Estimated to produce (in 1944)	£20,918
Rents (annually)	£177

These figures are taken from the statement of affairs produced by company secretary Ninian R. Davies and certified by him on 11 May 1944.

A. A. Thomas of Llandudno had been appointed liquidator on 17 March 1944 and took over responsibility for disposing of the assets. In his observations on the winding up the Official Receiver commented, 'It is clear that after payment of the receivership costs and expenses there will be a substantial deficiency on the debentures and there is no prospect of any funds becoming available in the liquidation for the unsecured creditors. The share capital of £90,000 has also been irretrievably lost.' With those stark remarks, that should have been the end of the Welsh Highland Railway.

Extract from Accounts, 1922-6

Year	Passenger receipts (£)	Goods etc receipts (£)	Revenue loss (£)	Net loss (£)	Total deficiency as on balance sheet (£)
1922	227	3,790	651	571	571
1923	2,462	3,635	1,573	1,484	2,056
1924	1,914	3,961	2,331	2,259	8,494
1925	1,089	3,987	742	675	13,443
1926	568	3,388	787	696	18,437

Locomotives and Rolling Stock

The WHR inherited two locomotives, *Moel Tryfan* and *Russell*, from the NWNGR, although strictly speaking the latter had been PBSSR property. *Moel Tryfan* was in poor condition and in need of attention. After being repaired, and cut down to fit the FR's loading gauge, it was used regularly on both railways until it entered Boston Lodge for repairs in 1934. As already stated, it passed to FR ownership following C. E. Davies's request to keep it in 1938. *Moel Tryfan* was cut up in 1954.

Russell became the locomotive most closely associated with the WHR. Before the 1924 season commenced, a poor attempt was made to reduce its stature to fit on the FR. Not only was the attempt futile but the locomotive's appearance was diminished too. *Russell* was painted green when the FR took over the WHR in 1934. In 1941 it was requisitioned and sold. First it went to the Brymbo Steel Co at Hook Norton in 1942, remaining there until 1948. Then it passed to B. Fayle & Co at Purbeck, where it stayed until 1953. The Industrial Railway Society acquired it for preservation in 1953 and it was moved to the Talyllyn Railway for restoration to museum display condition in 1955. In 1965 ownership passed to WHLR (1964). Restoration, including a new boiler and restoring its NWNGR profile, was completed at Gelert's Farm, alongside the WHR trackbed, in 1987.

To expand the WHR loco fleet, consideration was given to reacquiring *Gowrie*, then resident in a Darlington scrapyard. This opportunity was not taken up so Col Stephens encouraged the purchase, for £240, of an ex-WD World War 1 Baldwin 4-6-0T. Due to its size it was restricted to the WHR except for visits to Boston Lodge for maintenance or overnight lodging. At first painted black, the FR painted it red in 1934. The Welsh enginemen never got the measure of it and it was never named. It was requisitioned in 1941 and cut up the following year.

The WHR steam fleet was augmented as required by FR locomotives. It is reported that in 1923 Fairlies worked through to Dinas but otherwise only the Englands left the FR. McAlpine had hired *Palmerston* for a short time during the construction period.

Arising from Col Stephens's influence, the WHR saw the use of a former World War 1 armoured Simplex tractor from 1923. The *Railway Gazette* reported attending a series of tests on the WHR that year, saying that the locomotive 'may be useful for miscellaneous duties or special trips, or for light goods traffic'. The journal noted a lack of familiarity on the driver's part, remarking that the tractor 'acquitted itself well' during a journey from Dinas Junction to Porthmadog, via Bryngwyn. This locomotive is the FR's *Mary Ann*.

The FR obtained another former military locomotive in 1925, now *Moelwyn*. Following a suggestion that it would be suitable for hauling one-coach winter trains on the WHR, the 1918-built Baldwin petrol loco was equipped with vacuum brakes in 1928.

Also in 1928 Kerr Stewart loaned the WHR that company's first diesel locomotive for trials. This was a six-wheeled machine with a 60hp McLaren-Benz engine. After a period on the FR it was returned to its makers. The locomotive was later exported to the Union Vale sugar estate in Mauritius. Under the auspices of the Greenwich & District Narrow Gauge Society and the FR Trust, it was returned to the FR for preservation in 1997.

In 1934 the locomotive fleet was shown as three Locomotives named *Russell*, *Baldwin* and *Moeltryfan* (sic)!

Spring recorded the existence of 13 passenger coaches and a four-wheeled van at Dinas in 1921. The summer cars had been kept under cover at Dinas and were in relatively good condition having, naturally, only seen light summer use. Of the remainder, some required heavy repairs and most needed repainting. Dark green was the WHR livery. They all had their height reduced to enable them to work on the FR. Through working highlighted problems with non-matching couplings and brake gear that were eventually appropriately modified.

Six open Hudson toastrack coaches obtained by the FR in 1923 augmented the fleet. These were cheap and intended for use on both lines. The WHR was intended to pay its share but never did. By 1929 four had had their bodies removed. One of the corridor cars was converted to be a buffet car, first seeing use in this form in the 1928 season.

The 1934 lease identified the carriage stock thus:

3 Summer open cars; seating capacity 56 each
1 Corridor Coach; seating capacity 38
1 Corridor Coach; seating capacity 20
1 Inspection Saloon Coach; capacity 32
2 Composite Carriages, with 1 van compartment, 1 first class compartment, 2 third class compartments each; seating capacity 8 first class passengers, 16 third class passengers each coach.

The inspection saloon was the Gladstone Car. The FR painted the carriages different colours — green, blue, pink and red — apparently to make the operation more attractive to the public!

One of the 1894 Ashbury carriages passed to FR ownership, the remainder being sold or scrapped at Dinas in 1942. The restored Gladstone Car and the remains of the buffet car are in the possession of the WHLR (1964).

Dereliction, Dismantling & Scrapping

Below left:
Russell and the Baldwin inside Dinas loco shed in 1938.
W. A. Camwell/
Adrian Gray Collection

Right: By 1941 their plates had been removed. *WHR(P)*

Above: Carriages were left standing outside, as seen here in 1939. *A. E. Rimmer/WHR(P)*

Right: Bryngwyn station in 1941. *J. F. Bolton/WHR(P)*

left: The demolition contractor's train at Glan-yr-afon, 1941.
J. F. Bolton/WHR(P)

Below left: In the Aberglaslyn Pass, 1941.
J. F. Bolton/WHR(P)

Right: Tryfan Junction station and the demolition train, 1941.
J. F. Bolton/WHR(P)

Centre right: The demolition contractor's train at Snowdon Ranger, 1941.
J. F. Bolton/WHR(P)

Below: After the demolition of 1941, the Croesor Tramway section remained *in situ*. The Beddgelert siding is seen in 1947 with recently lifted rail being accumulated.
R. K. Cope/
Adrian Gray Collection

Above: Betws Garmon with Mynydd Mawr behind. The top of the typical NWNGR bowstring bridge, crossing the Afon Gwyrfai, is visible to the left of the derelict station building. *W. G. Rear Collection*

Left: In Dinas yard the buildings disintegrate and the trackbed returns to nature, date unknown. *Peter Johnson Collection*

Below left: Rhyd Ddu. The window and door frames and the refreshment room have all gone. *W. G. Rear Collection*

Right: Beddgelert in 1947, looking towards Porthmadog. *Real Photographs*

Centre right: River bridge at Hafod Garregog, Cnicht behind, 1947. *Real Photographs*

Below: Croesor Junction looking towards Porthmadog, 1947. *Real Photographs*

Left: Porthmadog looking towards Madoc Street, April 1974. The boundary between the FR and the WHR is behind the parked car. On the ground alongside the Britannia Foundry is the Baldwin's surviving water tank, now preserved by the Welsh Highland Railway Ltd at Gelert's Farm. This area is now the entrance to a supermarket, and the ground still, in 1998, belongs to the railway! *Peter Johnson*

Above: For a time during the 1960s the Welsh Highland Light Railway (1964) Co (now Welsh Highland Railway Ltd, WHR(P)) was allowed access to Beddgelert station site, storing track materials and some wagons there. *M. J. Bishop*

Right: WHR(P) commenced operations on the Beddgelert Siding site on 2 August 1980, using diesel power. Steam traction was introduced over the 1983 May Day holiday weekend. Peckett 0-4-2T *Karen* was built in 1942 and exported to the Rhodesia Chrome Mines Ltd. Arriving in Porthmadog in 1975, it was returned to working order at Gelert's Farm. *Karen* has been withdrawn awaiting overhaul since 1993. *Peter Johnson*

Welsh Highland Railway revival — to the Millennium

s far as can be ascertained, the first external proposal for the future of the WHR trackbed came in 1941. The Liverpool & District Ramblers' Federation circulated Caernarvonshire County Council and others proposing that the freehold should be acquired with a view to its dedication as a public footpath. When the local authorities expressed interest but unwillingness to offer financial support (hardly surprisingly) the Federation launched an appeal to raise £2,000 to be handed to Caernarvonshire County Council as an earnest of 'widespread desire to acquire this unique right of way'. Nothing more was heard of this proposal directly but the idea did not go away.

On the trackbed, the track on the Croesor Junction-Porthmadog section was dismantled in 1948/9, as was some of that at Hafod Ruffydd. The remnant of the Parliamentary Croesor

Tramway, parts of the non-statutory tramway and the Porthmadog link line between Madoc Street and the GWR were removed by 1950. The liquidator sold some land at and near Dinas. Dinas station site became a highways depot of the County Council, while the NWNGR shed site was taken over by the water authority, later shared by the National Rivers Authority.

Preservation for railway purposes was first mooted in 1961, with the establishment of a Welsh Highland Railway Society. Lacking access to any part of the trackbed, the society established a depot at Kinnerley, Shropshire, in 1963. Negotiations with the liquidator, whereby the trackbed would be bought for £850, failed with the death of the liquidator in September 1964, before contracts could be exchanged. The society had become incorporated as Welsh Highland Light Railway (1964) Ltd (WHLR [1964]) in January 1964.

Above: Following a protracted overhaul, on several different sites, *Russell* was returned to operating condition on 18 April, Easter Saturday 1987, restored to NWNGR profile. It ran in grey primer that year. Photographed on 18 July 1987. *Peter Johnson*

Below: The third steam locomotive to be returned to working order at Gelert's Farm was Bagnall 0-4-2T *Gelert*. It was photographed during a steam test on 19 August 1991. *Peter Johnson*

With the death of the liquidator, the Official Receiver, a government officer, took over the WHR liquidation. So far as the trackbed was concerned, his objective was to ensure that it would pass to a body with sufficient resources to take on the liabilities, so that it did not return to him via another bankruptcy. In choosing to take into account the wishes of the debenture holders, negotiations became complex and protracted. Progress suffered from a lack of consistent local authority policy with regard to the trackbed, a cautious Official Receiver and the fleeting interest of outsiders.

A move to Porthmadog was made in 1973, after the WHLR had reached agreement to buy the former Beddgelert Siding from British Railways. Adjacent land at Gelert's Farm was purchased in 1975. A depot was set up, a three-quarter-mile-long railway built and a Light Railway Order obtained in 1980. The first trains ran on 2 August that year, terminating at Pen-y-mount, alongside the Welsh Highland trackbed proper.

The Porthmadog base was created to be a springboard for future development once trackbed access could be obtained. Over the years substantial workshop and storage facilities have been established at Gelert's Farm. Locomotives are restored, overhauled and serviced there; the line's carriages have been built there, too. While it could be argued that little progress had been made, the WHLR (1964) succeeded in maintaining public awareness about the trackbed, prevented further sales and discouraged many incursions. This account of WHLR (1964) history, both in its dealings with the authorities and in its own development, is necessarily condensed.

Above: Russell and *Gelert* at Porthmadog on 1 May 1993. *Peter Johnson*

Right: Before celebrating its 90th birthday over the 1996 Spring Bank Holiday weekend, *Russell* underwent a 10-year overhaul that saw the restoration of some NWNGR features, including the boiler-top sandpot. Phil Tucker, then the company's CME, is seen on the footplate on 18 August 1996; he later went on to play a role in the construction of the Dinas-Caernarfon railway. *Peter Johnson*

Below right: At the end of a busy day that had seen all coaches brought into traffic, *Russell* heads for Pen-y-mount. 30 April 1997. *Peter Johnson*

Left: On 24/25 October 1998 the FR's *Palmerston* visited the WHR (Porthmadog) to participate in the railway's annual 'Dirty Chappies' weekend. It is seen at Pen-y-mount with WHR(P) volunteer Andy Blackwell at the controls on 25 October. *Peter Johnson*

In 1978 the WHLR (1964) succeeded in getting restoration to Pont Croesor, just over 1½ miles, included in the District Plan. Gwynedd County Council later formed a Welsh Highland Railway sub-committee to oversee matters relating to the trackbed. The sub-committee proposed that the council buy the assets from the Official Receiver for £1, taking responsibility for all liabilities, and leasing parts to the WHLR (1964) as that organisation developed the resources to expand. The council also proposed allocating parts of the trackbed for other recreational uses. Encouraged that good progress was being made with the Official Receiver, in 1988 a Light Railway Order application for the Pont Croesor section was made jointly with Gwynedd County Council; this Order has not been made. Unbeknown to the WHLR (1964), the Ffestiniog Railway Co had in 1987 taken an interest in the trackbed, making a secret bid to the Official Receiver to buy it.

The FR's interest became public, causing considerable controversy, and great dismay on the part of the WHLR (1964), in late 1989. Facing a severe lack of credibility, the FR eventually announced that its intention was to restore the complete railway, including the junction railways, and to extend to Caernarfon, fulfilling the ambitions of Spooner and others of over 100 years earlier. The justification for FR involvement could have been extracted from paragraph No 43 of Spring's 1921 report (Chapter 3). In the event the first construction actually took place between Dinas and Caernarfon — see Spring's paragraph No 30.

The FR's decision to commence work at the Caernarfon end was a response to the town's recognised status as a one-attraction tourist centre (Caernarfon Castle). It lacked anything to entice visitors to stay longer than the time needed to tour the castle, then attracting some 400,000 visitors a year. As a commercial centre it was in decline. The standard gauge trackbed to Afon Wen was, and is, part of the Lôn Eifion cycleway; as far as Dinas it could easily accommodate both cycles and trains and at Caernarfon the terminus could be very close to the castle. The argument was that many of the castle's visitors could easily be tempted to take a train ride if they heard or saw it during their visit.

An unsuccessful attempt was made by the Festiniog Railway to bring the original Welsh Highland Railway (Light Railway) Co out of receivership in 1991. The application was based on the work of a breakaway group of WHLR (1964) members, who had obtained possession of most of the WHR Co shares and debenture certificates, which they gave to the Festiniog Railway Trust. In turning down the application, the High Court judge suggested that the 1896 Light Railway legislation could be used to transfer the assets from the Official Receiver.

In 1992, therefore, the FR made a Light Railway Order application for powers to take over the remaining assets (and liabilities) of the old WHR Co from the Official Receiver. This was accompanied by an application for the Dinas-Caernarfon line. The WHLR (1964) and Gwynedd County Council jointly made competing applications and the matter inevitably went to a public inquiry, held the following year. Eventually the Secretary of State decided in favour of the FR and the transfer Order was made in 1995. The Welsh Highland Railway Society was formed to support the project in 1993.

Continued on page 100

The Millennium Railway

Right: Construction work on the Dinas-Caernarfon railway was formally started on 15 January 1997, with a ceremonial tape-breaking at Dinas. Performed by one of the contractor's excavators and the railway's Funkey diesel locomotive, the latter was the first motive power delivered for the new railway. *Peter Johnson*

Below: On the afternoon of 2 October 1997 the Funkey, *Castell Caernarfon*, hauled the first train of passenger stock to Caernarfon for test purposes. Members of HM Railway Inspectorate, ready to inspect the railway the following day, saw the train arrive at Caernarfon. *Peter Johnson*

Left: The same location in standard gauge days. The connection to the gas works siding and the Harbour Trustee's siding is on the right. *W. G. Rear*

Above: The first Garratt to arrive at Caernarfon was propelled there on 3 October 1997, to allow an inspector to assess visibility from the footplate. *Peter Johnson*

Below: Dinas station almost ready for opening, on 3 October. The Funkey stands in the platform with the first five coaches. *Peter Johnson*

Above: A very busy scene from the same vantage point in 1911. The LNWR 'Cauliflower' 0-6-0 stands at the same spot as the Funkey in the previous photograph. *Ian Allan Library*

Right: Back-up steam power was provided in the form of the Festiniog Railway's Alco, 2-6-2T *Mountaineer*. A test run with carriages, the first steam train to Caernarfon, was made on 4 October, seen between Coed Helen Road and St Helen's Road. *Peter Johnson*

Below right: The first run of Garratt 'NGG16' 2-6-2+2-6-2T No 138 under its own power at Bontnewydd on 4 October. At this point the Nantlle Tramway formation is out of view to the left. *Peter Johnson*

RHEILFFORDD FFESTINIOG RAILWAY

Gorsaf yr Harbwr · Harbour Station,
Porthmadog, Gwynedd. LL49 9NF
Ffôn/Tel: 01766 512340 · Ffacs/Fax: 01766 514576

RHEILFFORDD ERYRI WELSH HIGHLAND RAILWAY

**Mae rheilffordd newydd
Caernarfon wedi agor.
Caernarfon's new railway
has opened.**

**Bydd trenau'n rhedeg bob dydd
tan 2 Tachwedd.
Trains will be operating daily
until 2nd November.**

Bydd trenau'n cychwyn o Gaernafon i Dinas am:
Trains will depart Caernarfon for Dinas:

| 1000 | 1100 | 1200 | 1330 | 1430 | 1530 |

Bydd trenau'n cychwyn o Dinas am:
Return Trains will depart Dinas for Caernarfon:

| 1030 | 1130 | 1230 | 1400 | 1500 | 1600 |

Tâl arferol · Ordinary Fare £3.00

Gyda'r gostyngiadau arferol
Normal concessions apply

Above: Following a successful inspection and receipt of formal notification that passenger-carrying trains could be run, an unadvertised service was run on the weekend of 11/12 October, attracting large numbers, especially when word got around that the fare was only 50p! No 138 leaves Caernarfon on 12 October. *Peter Johnson*

Left: The timetable published for the 1997 service. During this short season there were empty stock workings from Dinas at 09.30 and from Caernarfon at 16.30. *Peter Johnson Collection*

Above right: The first occasion two Garratts were in steam at Caernarfon occurred on 18 October 1998, when No 143 was operated on test, double-headed with No 138. *Peter Johnson*

Right: On 19 October 1998, as part of the line's first enthusiast event, the only surviving de Winton locomotive in working order, 0-4-0VBT *Chaloner*, ran to Caernarfon and posed opposite the former de Winton works for photographs. *Peter Johnson*

Simultaneously with this high-profile legal work, consideration was being given to the operating requirements of the 25-mile-long railway. The criteria established to attract the sophisticated traveller of the 21st century were:

1. Speeds of up to 25mph to be the norm, with locomotives capable of good acceleration and with power to cope with gradients of up to 1 in 40, to give an acceptable journey time.
2. Trains of 10 or 12 cars hauled by a single loco.
3. High-quality coaches with all conveniences, catering etc.

A considerable amount of suitable equipment, in the form of locomotives, wagons and track materials, was found to be available from the Alfred County Railway and the Port Elizabeth Cement Works in South Africa. The locomotive requirement would be met by using Manchester-built 'NGG16' class 2-6-2+2-6-2 Beyer Garratts from the former line and a South African-built Funkey Bo-Bo 350hp diesel locomotive from the latter.

By 1995 the complete 25-mile railway project was priced at around £20 million. In October 1995 the Millennium Commission announced that it would make a £4.3 million contribution to the WHR from Lottery funding. This was 43% of the £9.1 million cost of building from Caernarfon to Rhyd Ddu, 12 miles, by the year 2000. Further grants were obtained from the European Regional Development Fund, the Welsh Development Agency and the Wales Tourist Board, representing 85% of the funding required for Caernarfon-Rhyd Ddu. Sponsorship of particular projects came from Historic Houses Hotels and First Hydro. By January 1997 over £1 million had been spent.

In 1996 the FR established the Welsh Highland Light Railway Co Ltd (WHLR). It has the task of building and equipping the new railway. The new company's first board meeting was held in December 1996, when one of its first actions was to appoint Roland Doyle as General Manager. At the same time Gwynedd Council, the unitary authority replacing the County Council, declared its support of the project by granting a 999-year lease on the Dinas-Caernarfon trackbed, the railway undertaking to rebuild the cycleway on this section. The former Dinas station site, a council road depot, was sold to the railway and the council also donated its WHR debentures.

Civil engineering contractor Mowlem received the £¾ million contract to clear the route,

renovate underbridges and culverts, install drainage and fencing, relocate and rebuild the cycle track, and ballast the formation. The contractor built the platforms at Dinas and Caernarfon, renewed the prop under the Coed Helen bridge near Caernarfon, and cleared the route for rail access into the old NWNGR yard at Dinas. Work started in January 1997.

The first track laying, in May 1997, was done by hand. A pair of unpowered rail movers was designed and built at Dinas, seeing considerable use thereafter. To deal with the track panels, a track-laying machine was commissioned from Winson Engineering. Certified as a crane and equipped with an air-powered lifting gantry, it needed a certain amount of tweaking before the gang got the measure of it. Use of the track-layer attracted more interest from local observers than any other construction activity; they sometimes congregated on the adjacent cycle track in crowds of up to 30 to see it in action. Track-laying was carried out by both paid staff and volunteers.

The track materials came from the 2ft gauge Donnybrook Railway in South Africa. It had been relaid with new materials just before it was closed due to a landslip. Enough was bought for Caernarfon-Betws Garmon and sidings, with delivery to Dinas beginning in September 1996.

The 18m (approx) lengths of 30kg/m (60lb) flat-bottom rail are laid on steel sleepers. Eighty lengths were supplied in complete panels. The remainder was not shipped in matching pairs of rails as ordered, so considerable time and effort had to be spent on rail sorting. The track fixings can be used in different combinations to allow for gauge widening on curves. These also needed considerable sorting: each sleeper requires one each of four different types of clip; bolts are both metric and imperial and come in two different sizes! Taking advantage of the African vacuum-braked bogie wagons, all works trains have continuous brakes. This practice will relieve the railway of the requirement to install trap points.

The platforms at Dinas are 200m long, for 15-car trains, and are located on the site of the former standard gauge station. Two parallel storage sidings alongside the platforms could become bay platform roads if there is demand for a Caernarfon shuttle service after the line is extended. A locomotive display shed is proposed for the site. Public facilities to be provided include conveniences, to be clad in a style that matches long-vanished buildings previously located on the platform, and further car parking — park-and-ride is likely to be a development here in the

Building the Line

Above: Clearance in progress at the Caernarfon end of Dinas station, 17 February 1997. *Peter Johnson*

future. A grant from the Welsh Development Agency for environmental improvements funded new entrance walling and fencing, car parking, a tarmac roadway and lighting standards on this site.

The south yard at Dinas includes the former NWNGR site. In 1950 it was acquired by the North West Wales River Authority, eventually passing to the Environment Agency. Extended in size during this period, the yard became surplus to Agency requirements in time to be reacquired for railway purposes. An existing shed on the site of the NWNGR carriage shed has been extended and furnished with a pit and wheel drop. Used as a running shed, it accommodates two Garratts. Another shed, located on the site of the NWNGR loco shed, has been equipped as a workshop. Rail access to this yard, and onto the NWNGR/WHR formation, from Dinas station is via the former standard gauge line, the overbridge on the old narrow gauge route having insufficient clearance for the new stock.

At Caernarfon the platform is designed for six-car trains. A portable building was installed for use as a booking office and shop. The restricted site in St Helen's Road is considered temporary by the railway, which will eventually need two 200m-long platforms and an engine release road. The exact location of the station will depend on local authority plans. If no further station space becomes available, a passing loop will be built outside the terminal, the formation being wide here as it originally accommodated parallel standard gauge lines.

With tracklaying completed in September 1997, the scene was set for the inspection. Garratt No 138 was delivered to Dinas in working order, as was back-up motive power, the FR's Alco 2-6-2T *Mountaineer*. The carriages were transported from Daventry and Minffordd. In the late afternoon of 2 October they were taken for their first run to Caernarfon, hauled by the Funkey. On arrival, there stood the HMRI inspection team: with Field Inspector Chris Parr were Peter Bridge, looking at crossings, and David Thornton, looking at track and structures. The next day they conducted a line inspection and examined the visibility from the locomotives. The certificate to operate arrived on 9 October. The Light Railway Order, likely to be the last for a Welsh railway, was made on 10 October. Trial running took place the same day, with an unadvertised service operated on the weekend of

Continued on page 104

Left: Building the station and using the trackbed as a dumper road, 1 April. The track panels stacked on the left were later laid between Pant Farm and Coed Helen.
Peter Johnson

Below left: A contrasting view taken on 30 July 1951.
H. B. Priestley/
W. G. Rear Collection

Above right: A works train powered by 39hp Hunslet *Harold,* on loan from Boston Lodge, on 30 July.
Peter Johnson

Centre right: The tracklaying gantry was brought into use to lay panels in August. It is seen in action near Hendy Crossing on the 25th. The gantry was designed and built to WHR requirements by Winson Engineering and mounted on a South African wagon chassis.
Peter Johnson

Below right: The former colliery ballast tamper being tested in Dinas station on 20 September.
Peter Johnson

Locomotives

11/12 October, attracting 300 passengers a day. The Mayor of Caernarfon performed the official opening on 13 October, followed by public running the next day. During the 22 operating days in 1997 9,200 passengers were carried, making 18,361 passenger journeys.

The initial service was promoted as a Caernarfon-based excursion, at £3 adult return, but it soon became clear that some people were using the train for shopping excursions from Dinas! Local residents with Festiniog railcards pay 75p for the return journey, slightly less than the parallel bus route. The line is marketed as Rheilffordd Eryri/Welsh Highland Railway.

The Festiniog Railway is responsible for running the trains, with all operating volunteers, engine crew and guards, having to be qualified on the FR. The Ffestiniog rulebook now has an appendix for the Welsh Highland section and WHR references appear in the FR's weekly notices. Trains run with a 'one engine in steam' staff, although radio control will be used in the future. WHR train control is at Porthmadog Harbour station.

Great interest, from enthusiasts and public alike, was taken in the performance of Garratt No 138, used on 19 of the 21 operating days in 1997 and during most of 1998. Crews soon developed finesse with it and competed with each other for lowest fuel consumption. Railway management was very impressed to learn that it was performing on £17.00 of fuel per trip. By contrast, the much smaller Alco, used on two days, cost £12.00 per trip. Running time is 12min from Caernarfon, 15min back, the increased running time being due to the cautious descent into Caernarfon.

Meanwhile, in April 1997 an application for a Transport & Works Order, deemed to be necessary for the reconstruction to take place, was submitted. The application triggered some remarkable about-turns from organisations previously supportive of the railway, including the Snowdonia National Park Authority and the National Trust. Indeed the objections received could be said to be reminiscent of those made to the PBSSR's 1903 application. Some objectors, including the Ramblers' Association nationally but not locally, called for the trackbed to be designated a footpath. The Ramblers' Association even went as far as applying for significant parts of the trackbed to be registered on the definitive footpath map; Gwynedd Council agreed with the FR's submission that a statutory railway, even one with no track, could not be registered as a footpath. Others were clearly using the railway as a means of obtaining unrelated political objectives. A public inquiry was held in Caernarfon in December 1997 and January 1998, considerably longer than those relating to the railway in 1921, 1922 and 1993. During the inquiry the FR reached an agreement with the WHLR (1964), by then renamed Welsh Highland Railway Ltd and claiming copyright on the name and objecting to the FR's application. The key point is that in exchange for withdrawing its objection, the WHLR (1964) will build to Pont Croesor, at its expense, when the Dinas-Waunfawr section is complete. Agreement was also reached concerning the use of the name, vintage train operation and for the WHLR (1964) to develop a WHR heritage centre at its Gelert's Farm site.

Subject to a successful outcome of the Transport & Works Order application, the railway will be opened in stages, first to Waunfawr and then Rhyd Ddu. The only change proposed to the formation will be lowering the trackbed through the overbridges, to be undertaken by contractors. The WHLR will act as main contractor. Sub-contractors will be

Continued on page 108

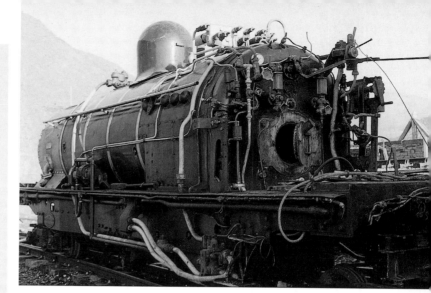

Far left: The bogie units of the two locomotives were unloaded at Minffordd Yard and ferried down to Boston Lodge by Hunslet 2-4-0STT *Linda*, the photograph, taken on 15 January 1997, demonstrating the contrasting size of the two types of locomotive. *Peter Johnson*

Above right: The first two South African 'NGG16' 2-6-2+2-6-2T Garratts arrived from the Alfred County Railway in January 1997. Both were in need of attention to bring them up to UK standards and to repair damage caused by sea water during the journey from Africa as deck cargo. The boiler unit of No 138 is seen here at the Festiniog Railway's Glan-y-pwll yard on 15 January. *Peter Johnson*

Centre right: No 140 arrived at Glan-y-pwll on 7 April. *Peter Johnson*

Below right: No 143 was reassembled at Dinas following repairs to boiler and bogies carried out by Ian Riley in Bury. It will retain its black SAR livery in recognition of its status as the last Garratt built at Beyer Peacock's Gorton works. It is seen, with No 138, at Caernarfon on 20 September 1998. The Dinas 'shed allocation' stickers affixed to the locomotives' buffer beams were obtained from the local Ford dealer who sticks them on to the cars he sells! *Peter Johnson*

Left: No 138 made its first public appearance in steam at Glan-y-pwll during the FR's 1997 gala. It is seen here shunting No 140 during pre-gala crew familiarisation on 2 May. *Peter Johnson*

Below left: No 138 on the climb out of Caernarfon towards the St Helen's Road bridge on 20 September 1998. The newly arrived Pullman car is coupled next to the locomotive. *Peter Johnson*

Above right: In 1998 the opportunity was taken to purchase two 'NG15' 2-8-2s Nos 133 and 134, as 'strategic reserve'. Another member of this class is located at the Gelert's Farm Works of WHR(P), where it has been dismantled for overhaul. No 133 was being shunted at Dinas on 21 September 1998. *Peter Johnson*

Centre right: The prototype Kerr Stewart diesel locomotive, tried out on the WHR in 1928, was returned to Wales from Mauritius in 1997 following the intervention of the Greenwich Narrow Gauge Society. Photographed in Minffordd Yard on 13 October 1997, plans are being made for its overhaul and demonstration on both the FR and WHR. *Peter Johnson*

Below right: The former Port Elizabeth cement works Funkey was overhauled at Boston Lodge, the work being completed in April 1996. Dafydd Wigley MP named it *Castell Caernarfon* at Caernarfon, during the town's annual carnival, on 26 July, the diesel travelling there by road. It was photographed at Hendy Crossing on 3 October 1997. *Peter Johnson*

responsible for fencing and clearance. Tracklaying will be by direct labour and volunteers. A further temporary terminus at, say, Beddgelert, will depend upon agreement of the National Park Authority. Completion to Porthmadog by 2005 is the overall objective.

A further public inquiry took place in July 1998, considering inter alia the Snowdonia National Park Authority's proposal to withdraw support for the WHR from its structure plan. It emerged that the Authority had changed its mind about the railway when responding to a personal objection made by the chairman of the Authority's planning committee!

Operation of Dinas-Caernarfon during 1998 continued to attract attention, although patronage was not as high as forecast due to a downturn in Welsh tourism generally. As a rule, if Caernarfon Castle was busy then the trains were busy. During the year, finishing-off work saw a water tank installed at Caernarfon, replacing temporary facilities at Dinas, the restoration of the NWNGR Dinas station building and construction of a 12-car carriage shed. Participants on a Gwynedd Council training scheme made the window frames for the station building. Following receipt of a petition from residents, a halt has been built at Bontnewydd, opening early in the 1999 season. Preparation for the future saw points manufactured for installation at Waunfawr.

The new railway's first enthusiast event took place on 19/20 September 1998, introducing Garratt No 143 and the new Pullman car to an admiring public, both performing their test trips along the line only the day before! Double-heading of the Garratts provided the spectacle of 164 tons of narrow gauge super-power in action.

Locomotives visiting for the event were 0-4-0STT *Palmerston* from the FR and de Winton 0-4-0VBT *Chaloner* and Hunslet 0-4-0ST *Alice*, both based at the Leighton Buzzard Railway in Bedfordshire. *Palmerston* was used on the 'old' WHR; *Chaloner* was built in Caernarfon, in workshops located opposite the new station, and worked in the Pen-yr-orsedd Quarry in the Nantlle vale, served by the Nantlle Tramway. *Alice* represented this popular locomotive class, once a common sight in North Wales. During the weekend the three performed drive-an-engine sessions at Dinas; on Saturday evening they ran solo light engine trips to Caernarfon, posing for photographs. Those who saw it will long remember the sight of *Chaloner* opposite the de Winton factory.

The completed Welsh Highland Railway will be like no other. The terms preservation and heritage, as in 'preserved railway' or 'heritage railway', will only be applied to it with some difficulty. It could be said that all that is being preserved is the route and some buildings, for the carriages are all new and the locomotives will be workhorses, intended to be master of the job and then some. The railway will be a major part of the transport infrastructure in this part of North Wales and the Snowdonia National Park, providing a useful 25-mile off-road link between Caernarfon and Porthmadog.

Locomotives and rolling stock

The first motive power obtained for the WHR was a Funkey Bo-Bo diesel locomotive obtained from the Port Elizabeth Cement Co and delivered to the FR in 1993, in company with a second for the FR. These South African-built locomotives have 350hp Cummins engines that have seen very little use. Delivered, each cost £5,000 plus £6,000 carriage. Named *Castell Caernarfon*, the WHR's was overhauled at Boston Lodge and delivered to Dinas for the start of work in 1997. It saw occasional use during the construction phase, serves as back-up to the steam locomotives and will be used for off-peak services.

Two 'NGG16' 2-6-2+2-6-2 Beyer Peacock Garratts were obtained from the Alfred County Railway at a cost of £90,000 each overhauled. Numbered 138 and 143, the latter was the last Garratt built in Manchester. Their boiler units arrived at the FR's Glan-y-pwll yard on 14 January 1997, their bogies going to Boston Lodge for attention to bearings, bushes and lubrication. Despite work undertaken in South Africa, both locomotives required additional work to be carried out to bring them up to UK standards. No 143's boiler and both its bogies received attention at Ian Riley's works in Bury. No 138 was first steamed at Glan-y-pwll in time for display at the FR's 1997 gala and transferred to Dinas just prior to the October opening. Its livery is a rich green. No 143 was first steamed on 18 September 1998; it is to retain its SAR black livery in view of its historic significance. Both locomotives have been converted to burn oil.

A third Garratt, the red-liveried No 140, was offered to the project for a nominal £100 by a group of German enthusiasts. It arrived at Glan-y-pwll for the WHR in April 1997; delivered unrestored, it will be put back into working order at a later date. Three more Garratts have been earmarked for future acquisition.

In 1998 two unrestored South African Franco-Belge 'NG15' 2-8-2s, Nos 133 and 134, were obtained from the proprietor of an abandoned project for a proposed tourist railway in Yorkshire.

The first Garratt built, K1, is owned by the Festiniog Railway Trust. Built in 1909, it was reacquired by Beyer Peacock from its Tasmanian owners in 1947 and bought by the FR in 1966. Too large for the FR's loading gauge, it was displayed at the National Railway Museum from 1979 until 1995. It is being overhauled for the WHR at the Birmingham Railway Museum and should be capable of dealing with light (!) trains at line speed. Funded by donations and covenants, over £90,000 of the £120,000 needed for restoration has been raised.

For the completed railway a fleet of 60 coaches is predicted. Winson Engineering at Daventry received the £400,000 contract for the first six, estimated to be adequate for the Dinas-Caernarfon service. They consist of a brake/saloon composite with wheelchair access (27 seats), three open saloons (36 seats), an open (36 seats) and a 'Pullman'. Winson also overhauled the South African wagon bogies for the passenger stock, downrating the springing and adding bolsters and shock absorbers. The open was delivered to the FR for trials in July 1997, the four saloons going directly to Dinas that October. Named *Bodysgallen*, the Pullman was delivered in September 1998. One metre longer than the 12m saloons, giving passengers more legroom, it will be used for high-quality dining services. The open has already proved to be popular; on some of the more lightly loaded trains it was sometimes the only carriage in use, even when raining! First Hydro, operators of Dinorwic power station, sponsored the brake/saloon, and Historic Houses Hotels, operators of the Bodysgallen Hall Hotel near Llandudno, sponsored the Pullman.

The coaches were designed by Winson to meet the FR's concept and the saloons must be the most sophisticated carriages ever put into service on a UK narrow gauge railway. Features include quality timber lining, double-glazing, oil fired heating, public address, stainless steel body frames and axle-driven alternators. In summer passengers should appreciate the heating equipment operating as a forced-air ventilation system. The livery is the same as the FR's; internally the seats are covered with hard-wearing moquette woven with an FR/WHR motif. Although larger than Ffestiniog stock, these carriages will fit the FR loading gauge except at Garnedd Tunnel.

A fleet of South African wagons, both dropsides and flats, has been obtained for works/construction use. The former Lodge Hill & Upnor Military Railway 'Combination car' is being converted for use as a mess car on construction trains. D. Wickham & Co of Ware built it in 1957 as a brake coach with separate compartments for officers and 'other ranks'. The Welshpool & Llanfair Light Railway obtained it in 1961 and it was among the first carriages used there on reopening in 1963. It was sold on to the South Tynedale Railway in 1988. It arrived at Dinas after a period with a contractor in November 1998.

Equipment used during tracklaying included the Funkey, 39hp Hunslet diesel *Harold* (on temporary loan from Boston Lodge) and Planet *Upnor Castle*, sold to the WHLR by the FR. A former NCB tamping machine, of minimal proportions for use underground, was obtained from the Yorkshire Engine Co.

Carriages

Left: For the 1997/8 service Winson Engineering Ltd supplied five coaches built to the railway's specifications. Three of the vehicles, two open saloons and the brake composite, were photographed in the company's Daventry works on 17 July 1997. A glimpse of the third open saloon can be seen through the door at the back. It is intended that the railway will eventually have a fleet of about 50 carriages.
Peter Johnson

Centre left: In September 1998 Winson Engineering delivered a Pullman car. Named *Bodysgallen*, its construction was sponsored by Historic Houses Hotels Ltd, operators of the Bodysgallen Hall Hotel near Llandudno. Photographed on 20 September 1998, *Bodysgallen* is intended to be part of a wine and dine operation; in the meantime passengers pay a £3 supplement, in addition to the £3 return fare, to ride in it.
Peter Johnson

Below left: The first of the new vehicles to be completed was the open, delivered to the FR in July 1997 with the intention that it should undergo riding trials on the Minffordd shuttle service. Regrettably the letter giving authorisation for restricted use did not arrive from HM Railway Inspectorate until the beginning of October, so it spent most of the time at Boston Lodge getting in the way! Photographed on 30 July.
Peter Johnson

Parliamentary Powers

The following Acts and Orders have authorised various stages in the development of the railway route between Porthmadog and Caernarfon or influenced that development:

Nantlle Railway Act 1825 (Incorporation and power to build 'a railway or tramroad from a quarry called Gloddfarlon, in the parish of Llandwrog, to the town and port of Carnarvon');

Nantlle Railway Act 1827 (For additional funds);

Nantlle Railway Act 1828 (For additional time);

Carnarvonshire Railway Act 1862 (Incorporation with powers to build a railway 'between Carnarvon and Port Madoc');

Carnarvon & Llanberis Railway Act 1864 (Incorporation, power to build, power to use part of Carnarvonshire Railway and to use joint station at Caernarfon);

Croesor and Portmadoc Railway Act 1865 (Authorising the carriage of passengers on the Croesor Tramway and an extension of it from Portmadoc to Borth-y-gest);

Beddgelert Railway Act 1865 (For making a railway from Portmadoc to Beddgelert);

Nantlle Railway Act 1865 (To widen and extend and to raise additional capital);

Carnarvon & Llanberis Railway Extension Act 1865 (Further powers, deviation to join with Bangor & Carnarvon Railway at Caernarfon, branch to Betws Garmon Valley);

Beddgelert Railway (Extension and Deviation) Act 1866 (Extension to Llyn Gwynant);

Carnarvon & Llanberis Railway Act 1867 (LNWR to be joint owner, to subscribe, extension of time, and repeal of articles concerning joint station in 1864 Act);

Carnarvonshire Railway (Nantlle Railway Transfer) Act 1867 (Dissolution of Nantlle Railway Co and power to divert a road);

Gorsedda (sic) Junction and Portmadoc Railways Act, 1872 (Permitting inter alia the Gorseddau Tramway to connect to and make use of part of the Croesor Tramway);

North Wales Narrow Gauge Railways Act 1872 (Incorporating the NWNGR and other purposes);

North Wales Narrow Gauge Railways (Lease) Act 1873 (Enabling the NWNGR to lease the Moel Tryfan Undertaking);

North Wales Narrow Gauge Railways Act 1876 (Abandonment of Railway No 1 (the General Undertaking) and raising additional capital);

Portmadoc, Croesor and Beddgelert Tram Railway Act (Authorising construction of a railway between the Croesor Tramway and Beddgelert);

North Wales Narrow Gauge Railways (Extensions etc) Act 1885 (Authorising construction of a railway from Dinas to Caernarfon and other lines);

North Wales Narrow Gauge Railways Act 1890 (Extension of time for undertaking works authorised in the 1885 Act and other purposes);

North Wales Narrow Gauge Railways (Beddgelert Light Railway Extension) Order 1900 (Construction of a railway between South Snowdon and Beddgelert);

Portmadoc, Beddgelert & South Snowdon Railway Act 1901 (Sanctioning the sale of the Croesor Tramway to the PBSSR Co and authorising the construction of a branch line at Porthmadog and a line to Beddgelert);

North Wales Electric Power Act 1904 (Incorporation of NWPTC and transfer of PBSSR Co's electricity generating powers authorised in 1901 Act);

Portmadoc, Beddgelert & South Snowdon Railway Act 1904 (Authorising the construction of a narrow gauge railway between Dinas and Caernarfon);

North Wales Narrow Gauge Railways (Light Railway) Order 1905 (Authorising the working and maintenance of the Moel Tryfan Undertaking of the NWNGR as a light railway);

Portmadoc, Beddgelert & South Snowdon Railway (Beddgelert Light Railway Extension) Order, 1906 (Authorising the abandonment of part of the railway sanctioned by the North Wales Narrow Gauge Railways [Beddgelert Light Railway Extension] Order 1900 and its replacement and the transfer of powers granted in that Order from the NWNGR to the PBSSR);

Portmadoc, Beddgelert & South Snowdon Railway (Light Railway Extension at Carnarvon) Order, 1908 (Deviation of 1904 railway at Caernarfon);

Portmadoc, Beddgelert & South Snowdon Railway (Light Railway) Order, 1908 (Powers to work the railways authorised by the 1901 and 1904 Acts as a light railway and to build a railway between Beddgelert and Betws-y-coed);

Welsh Highland Railway (Light Railway) Order 1922 (Authorising the incorporation of the WHR (LR) Company and other purposes);

Welsh Highland Railway (Light Railway) Amendment Order 1923 (Authorising variation of routes near Beddgelert);

Festiniog Railway (Light Railway) Order 1923 (The FR to be worked as a light railway and to construct a railway to connect to the WHR at Porthmadog);

The Beddgelert Siding Light Railway Order 1980 (WHLR [1964] Co Order);

The Welsh Highland Railway (Transfer) Light Railway Order 1995 (Authorising the transfer of the assets of the Welsh Highland Railway (Light Railway) Co from the receiver to the FR Co);

The Caernarfon Light Railway Order 1997 (Authorising the Dinas-Caernarfon railway).

THE WAY AHEAD

Above: The tunnel under the A487 road at Dinas on 24 March 2000, looking towards Porthmadog. The cutting on the far side has been cleared and work is progressing in building a new floor at a lower level to accommodate the higher locomotives and rolling stock on the revived railway. *Peter Johnson*